THAT WE MAY SHARE HIS HOLINESS

A Fresh Approach
to church Discipline

TOMMY SOUTH

*"He disciplines us for our good,
that we may share His holiness."*
HEBREWS 12:10

BIBLE GUIDES

P.O. Box 273
Abilene, Texas 79604-0273

To Linda,
whose disciplined Christian life is a model for my own
and for those of many others.
With loving appreciation in the thirtieth year of our marriage.

Copyright 1997 by James T. South. All rights reserved.
Library of Congress Catalog Card Number: 97-73585
ISBN 0-9623723-1-0

CONTENTS

PREFACE

"Church discipline." The mere mention of the words brings a host of reactions, from interest to agitation. The concept has always been there in the collective consciousness of the church, because it keeps coming up in the pages of the New Testament. Still, we've never quite known what to do with it. Is it a positive thing, or negative? Will it help, or hurt? Is it a commandment which we must simply fulfill with gritted teeth, regardless of the consequences? Is it a "tool for church growth"? Or does it have a deeper significance, and perhaps benefits which we haven't considered?

I've written this book in the conviction that what we need is, as the sub-title suggests, a fresh approach to church discipline. Somehow the approaches of the past have not worked. Not that there hasn't been some truth and value in them, but they haven't motivated us to be a disciplining people.

That fresh approach is, I'm convinced, found in the pages of the Bible. It isn't to be found in new theories or techniques that we devise, but in listening to Scripture afresh, in letting the inspired writers tell us what discipline should be all about, and trusting their guidance absolutely. This book is an attempt to help us see what the Bible has really been saying all along.

Others have, of course, written on this subject, although the literature is not particularly large.[1] Some of it is to be found in books written on a popular level, but much valuable material is contained in numerous commentaries and scholarly articles on the relevant texts. Rather than offer a bibliography which would be either incomplete or ponderously long, I refer the reader to the notes at the end of each chapter.

No one writes a book alone, and this one is certainly no exception. My thinking has been sharpened through the presentation of some of this material in Bible classes, sermons, lectureships, and preachers' meetings. To every one whose questions, comments, and encouragements have spurred me to press further, I owe a debt I cannot adequately repay.

Several people have read all or portions of this manuscript at various stages, and their suggestions have been invaluable, even when they could not be incorporated. These include my wife, Linda, Pat Langston, Mural Worthey, Robert Oglesby, Philip Slate, Tom Olbricht, and Harvey and Sue Porter. Neil Lightfoot read everything with his customary thoroughness, and caused this to be a much better book than it would be otherwise. My thanks also to Flavil Yeakley, Jr., Jimmy Jividen, and Howard Norton for furnishing me with information and suggestions which I have incorporated in various ways. Each one has provided a special form of fellowship for which I thank God, and none is responsible for the shortcomings of this book.

My prayer is that you, the reader, will be led to a new appreciation of God's discipline, through a renewed understanding of his word.

1. A welcome recent addition to the literature is the section on discipline in Everett Ferguson, *The Church of Christ: A Biblical Ecclesiology for Today* (Grand Rapids: Eerdmans, 1996) 373-89.

"Discipline is a Thing so little known to us, and that of the Primitive Church hath hitherto lain involved in such a Number of voluminous Writers, that the drawing it thence into a clear and open Light, would, I conceived, be a Thing of much Use and Benefit: So that if I have performed this Part well and faithfully, I am not without Hope, that I have done a good Work. Whether I have so performed, or not, the Reader must judge for himself upon Tryal made of it."

— Nathaniel Marshall, *The Penitential Discipline of the Primitive Church*, 1714

INTRODUCTION

WHAT'S WRONG WITH THIS PICTURE?

It has been twenty-five years since anyone was publicly disciplined at the Blank Street Church of Christ. The last time, it was a prominent member who had left his wife for his secretary and so embarrassed the church that *something* had to be done.

That was twenty-five years ago. Now, the Blank Street church has a new preacher, and he's been preaching some sermons on church discipline and has convinced the elders of their neglect in not practicing it. In a recent meeting the elders voted to begin disciplining the erring according to Biblical guidelines and agreed on the following procedures:

1. They would go back over the membership rolls of the last twenty-five years and compile a list of all who were still living in their community but were no longer attending worship.

2. Each person on the list would be visited by the elders and admonished to repent and make a public acknowledgment of his/her unfaithfulness.

3. Following this visit, each person on the list would be sent

a letter repeating the plea to repent and advising that those failing to do so would have their names read before the church in two weeks.

4. All who failed to respond before the two weeks were up would have their names put before the church, and everyone would be admonished to call or visit the offenders and urge them to come back to the Lord.

5. After two more weeks, all who refused the appeals of their brethren would be formally withdrawn from by the church and their names would be removed from the church roll.

So the elders set about their task. At first there was a spirit of enthusiasm among the elders and one of bemused curiosity among the members. But by the time the letters were mailed, there were beginning to be some rumbles, especially from members whose close friends and relatives were being threatened with public discipline. (There was no such uneasiness about some on the list, because only a few remembered who they were.) At one elders' meeting there was even heated discussion about the way some of the visits had been handled, especially where friends and relatives of the elders were involved. When the list of names was read in the assembly two weeks later, there was outright hostility against the elders, who were accused by some of having ulterior motives and of needing to get their own houses in order. And, of course, there was hostility against the preacher for bringing all of this up in the first place.

Finally, the day arrived. One of the elders, with much emotion in his voice, expressed the regret of the church at having to withdraw from several erring members — which included practically everyone on the original list — and the names were read one by one.

By this time there was considerable tension among the congregation, aggravated by a wide range of emotions. Some threatened to leave. Others vowed to ignore the elders' instructions and associate with the disciplined just as they had always done. Others were relieved and gratified that, after all these years, the right thing had finally been done. But everyone was disturbed that the whole affair had created so much strife within the congregation.

After several weeks most of the emotion had subsided, but the tension was still there. Two families did leave and started attending elsewhere. The anger of others was gradually replaced by a deep sense of resentment toward the elders. A few months later one person on the list was restored, and the elders and preacher were gratified that their efforts had borne fruit. After about a year, however, the preacher, feeling that he had lost his effectiveness as a result of the resentment toward him, moved on. Gradually, the whole incident was forgotten, except by those who were still resentful.

Twenty-five years later, a new preacher came to the Blank Street church and began to preach about discipline. . . .

This scenario does not describe any particular church or incidence of church discipline. If it sounds familiar, it is because it is a composite of how I have generally witnessed the practice of discipline in churches of Christ over the past twenty-five years. It also reflects what many others have told me of their own experiences. So, chances are, if you have been in the church very long and have witnessed any discipline at all, you saw it done (or heard of it being done) something like this.

What's wrong with this picture? Lots of things actually, and in the course of this book I'll attempt to point out some of them. But the main thing wrong is that it shows, in spite of Biblical teaching, that (1) we haven't practiced discipline with any consistency, and (2) when we have, our efforts have been almost entirely without positive effect.

At this point let me hasten to say that I write this as a lover of the church and not as a critic. But because of our enormous failures in this area, it will be necessary to speak frequently in the negative. But whenever I must do so, it is always with a positive intent. And when I speak of "us" or "we," I mean it literally. Just before beginning this book, I was explaining my plan for the project to a preacher friend. He asked, in all seriousness, "Is discipline your area of expertise?" I explained that, although I had written a doctoral dissertation on the subject,

I did not consider myself an "expert" at all. I fear that discipline has not been practiced consistently enough among us for any of us to claim that title. Where such delicate issues as sin, redemption, individual spirituality, and the health of the church are concerned, there are no experts, only fellow strugglers.

We have always recognized the necessity for "positive" or what is sometimes called "preventive" discipline. Most congregations recognize the need for study of the word, regular worship, prayer, and the exhortation and admonition of godly leaders. This is all "disciplinary" in its own way, and no one would underestimate its importance. But "corrective" or "remedial" discipline is, for most of us, an enigma rather than a conviction and an established practice. Few among us would question that it is a thoroughly Biblical practice: it was taught by our Lord and widely practiced in the early church. Yet there has been a long, slow silence among us where discipline is concerned. We're a restorationist people, and to the extent that we are true to that ideal, we search the Scriptures to determine the Lord's will, then make the necessary changes and adjustments in order to do it. No one can decree these changes for all of us. We must individually and as congregations of God's people find them for ourselves. For this reason change for us generally comes about slowly (which isn't as bad as we impatient mortals sometimes believe). But in the area of discipline, we've been strangely content not to restore. In fact, in spite of the clarity with which the Bible speaks about discipline, many of our number actually are vocally opposed to the practice — and for the most part, there doesn't seem to be much alarm about this. We've become dangerously comfortable with our disobedience. My prayer is that this book will help in some small way to correct this.

But I don't by any means conceive of this as a negative work. To the contrary, I want to begin by attempting to provide what often has been lacking on this important subject: a solid Biblical and theological base for the practice of discipline. For this reason the following chapters contain some detailed studies of the various Biblical texts. While I have tried to keep these from becoming overly-technical, I have sought to examine them closely enough to see what they actually say (and don't say), and to see how each can help us deal with the practical realities of discipline among God's people today.[1] The various conclusions reached in this study arise from the texts themselves and build upon one another. It is, therefore, best to read the chapters in order.

Perhaps it's necessary at the outset to be clear regarding what this book is *not* about. In the early 1980s church discipline was a "live" topic among churches of Christ as a result of the highly-publicized case of Marian Guinn *vs.* the Collinsville, Oklahoma, Church of Christ. Ms. Guinn sued the congregation and its elders as a result of their disciplinary action due to her sexual immorality.[2] There was considerable apprehension on the part of church leaders all across the country, since the congregation was sued for a considerable sum of money, and lost the initial case. A portion of that decision was eventually overturned by the Oklahoma Supreme Court, but the Collinsville church ended up settling out of court for an undisclosed sum. As a result, there were numerous workshops and lectureship classes on the legal issues surrounding church discipline, and what churches and church leaders could do to protect themselves against such disasters as that experienced by the Collinsville church. In short, what happened was that many in our brotherhood became "legal experts" on the subject of discipline without first being adequately informed about and firmly committed to Biblical teaching regarding discipline. It was an ironic scenario: churches everywhere were protecting themselves against the legal consequences of practices in which most of them never engaged! The sad outcome was that more church leaders than ever became convinced of the inadvisability of practicing church discipline.[3]

You will not find any discussion of the legal issues surrounding discipline in this study. Such concerns are real, and I intend in no way to detract from the integrity or intentions of those who have explored them. But it has been a sad case of putting the cart before the horse. First, we must understand what the Lord's will is for the churches and commit ourselves to that.

There may *be* serious consequences to discipline — legal, financial, and otherwise — but then, there have always been serious consequences of taking God at his word. It is time that we devote ourselves as seriously to finding out what Scripture says about discipline as we have previously been devoted to protecting ourselves from its consequences.

Some may be disappointed in this book because it does not provide specific procedural suggestions for carrying out discipline. You will not find here any lists of "steps" to be followed, except those specified in particular New Testament texts. Part of our difficulty with discipline has been that we have sought to carry it out according to such lists, rather than prayerfully searching the Scriptures and being guided by the principles it provides. It is my conviction, based on these texts, that the Bible offers no such lists, because we are to deal with each situation and each person directly, lovingly, and as circumstances require — not according to any manual or handbook.

My prayer is that this book will be of help to every Christian who reads it. Even though I have addressed it specifically to the brotherhood of churches of Christ, it will hopefully be of interest to all who are interested in what the Bible has to say. But I have a special concern for the godly elders and preachers of the church who usually shoulder the burden of leading, shepherding, and disciplining God's people. If this work gives them even a small measure of the teaching, encouragement, and inspiration that they need in order to lead the church in discipline, I will be deeply grateful.

1.   For the more technical issues concerning these texts, the reader is referred to the various commentaries cited in later chapters, and to James T. South, *Disciplinary Practices in Pauline Texts* (Lewiston, N.Y.: Mellen Biblical Press, 1992).

2.   For details of this case, see Flavil R. Yeakley, Jr., "Implications for Church Discipline in the Case of Guinn vs. the Collinsville Church of Christ," a paper presented at the Conference on the Rule of Christ, Goshen College, Goshen, Indiana, 1992. Also, various articles and editorials in *The Christian*

Chronicle (April, 1984).

3. For documentation of the effects of the Collinsville case on brotherhood thinking about discipline, see Robert E. Whiddon, Jr., "The Current Status of the Practice of Church Discipline in the Churches of Christ in America" (Unpublished Ph.D. dissertation, Trinity Theological Seminary, 1996).

"To cut off an offender is good; to cure him, is better; but to prevent him falling, is best of all."
— Alexander Campbell, *The Christian System*

HOLINESS: THE REAL PURPOSE OF DISCIPLINE

One of the primary reasons why discipline has never found its rightful place among us and is even opposed by a significant number of Christians is that we have failed to see it in its proper theological context. How does discipline fit into the larger framework of Biblical revelation? How does it relate to other important Biblical themes? Traditionally, we have thought of discipline as arising out of a smattering of isolated, arbitrary commands. And when we have taught on the subject, it has too frequently been in a "proof-text" fashion, quoting the relevant texts without regard to their immediate contexts in the writings in which they occur or in the wider context of the Bible in general. As a result, we have presented discipline as something which the church must do in order to "be Scriptural," but there has been little understanding of *why* Scripture says what it does, and our people have remained largely unconvinced of the importance of discipline. Clearly, we must go deeper into the word in order to understand its significance.

God is never arbitrary; there is always a purpose behind his words. Sometimes he chooses to let us in on his reasoning, and sometimes he keeps that from us (Deuteronomy 29:29). In the case of discipline in the church, we are told, although we have generally overlooked the explanation. Discipline, the writer of Hebrews tells us, arises out of *the very nature of God himself*. We must be disciplined so that we will become more like God. And this aspect of his nature toward which we must be led can be summarized in one word: *holiness*.

Holiness in Hebrews

"Holiness" is not a very popular concept among us. Frequently we think of holiness as those things which we do *not* do, our isolation from the world and "worldly" things. But this is only one aspect of holiness. Left to this definition, we would become monks in the monastery rather than lights in the world. We may even shy away from the idea of holiness because of the connotation of "holier than thou" and the implication of spiritual arrogance. Then there is the frequent misunderstanding that holiness is an achievement, something we accomplish for ourselves by doing good.

To understand holiness properly, we must begin not with ourselves, but with *God*, whose essential nature is holiness. Holiness as applied to God describes his "differentness," his uniqueness. He is, as Rudolf Otto described him, "the Wholly Other,"[1] the one who is all that we are not and who exists in utter perfection. In Isaiah's vision of the Lord, the seraphim called out, "Holy, holy, holy is the Lord of hosts; the whole earth is full of his glory" (Is. 6:3). So deeply was Isaiah impressed by this vision of God that he calls him "the Holy One of Israel" some twenty-six times.

The Christians to whom Hebrews was originally written were in grave danger of giving up their faith in Christ and reverting to their former Jewish religion. Apparently as a result of discouragement, persecution, and a failure to appreciate the uniqueness of their Savior, they were contemplating trading their new faith for the old (some had already done so — 10:24-25). One way in which the author seeks to bolster their shaking faith is by pointing out to them the uniqueness of Jesus and of all that is connected with him. This is where the concept of holiness comes in: what Jesus brought to them came from the all-holy God and cannot be abandoned or taken lightly.[2]

Stephen Neill has aptly described Hebrews as "a letter which contains in germ everything that needs to be said about [holiness]."[3] The readers themselves are called "holy brethren" (3:1) and "saints" ("holy ones" — 6:10, 13:24), and the writer stresses that they have been "sanctified" ("made holy") by the blood of Christ (2:11, 9:13, 10:10, 10:14, 13:12), and warns them that turning away from Christ means profaning the blood of the convenant by which they had been sanctified (10:29). There is frequent reference to the "Holy" Spirit (2:4, 3:7, 9:8, 10:15). Jesus ministers in the true "sanctuary" ("holy place") versus the old earthly one (8:2, 9:1-3, 9:12, 9:24-25, 10:19, 13:11). And Jesus himself is said to be our high priest, "holy (*hosios*),[4] blameless, unstained, separated from sinners, exalted above the heavens" (7:26). If there is any question in our minds about the meaning of "holiness" for the people of God, Hebrews 7:26 should answer it. We are called on to be like our Lord: "blameless, unstained, separated from sinners." "So Jesus also suffered outside the gate in order to sanctify the people through his own blood. Therefore let us go forth to him outside the camp, and bear the abuse he endured" (13:12-13).

But Hebrews goes even further. We are not only called to be holy, our holiness is absolutely imperative: "Strive for peace with all men, and for the *holiness, without which no one will see the Lord*" (12:14). To fail to attain holiness is to "fail to obtain the grace of God," to become "defiled," "irreligious," and "immoral" (12:15-16).

> For you have not come to what may be touched, a blazing fire, and darkness, and gloom, and a tempest, and the sound of a trumpet, and a voice whose words made the hearers entreat that no further messages be spoken to them. . . . But

you have come to Mount Zion and to the city of the living God, the heavenly Jerusalem, and to innumerable angels in festal gathering, and to the assembly of the first-born who are enrolled in heaven, and to a judge who is God of all, and to the spirits of just men made perfect, and to Jesus, the mediator of a new covenant, and to the sprinkled blood that speaks more graciously than the blood of Abel. See that you do not refuse him who is speaking" (12:18-25).

This business of "holiness" is of vastly greater importance than we have often realized!

Yet exactly here we are faced with a problem: How can we, who are sinful, ever be holy?

The solution begins with the reality that Jesus, our High Priest, is holy (7:26). And, as Hebrews explains, by the shedding of his blood, we are *made* holy, much as the sprinkling with blood made holy the vessels in the temple (9:13, 10:10, 10:14, 13:12). So holiness (sanctification) is, in one sense, a gift which God gives us when we are baptized into Christ.

Still, we are called on in Hebrews to *be* holy and to *strive* for holiness, indicating that there is something lacking in our holiness, that it is somehow incomplete. But this is not unique to Hebrews. In several of his letters, Paul follows the pattern known as the *indicative* followed by the *imperative*. He states what we *are* as a result of being in Christ, then tells us what we must *do* in order to act out what we are and become even more so. For example, in Ephesians 1-3, Paul says that we are in Christ, saved by grace, and are the "new humanity" created by the cross. Then, in 4:1 he says, "I therefore . . . beg you to lead a life worthy of the calling to which you have been called," and proceeds in the rest of the letter to outline specifically what that entails. So we *are* holy through the blood of Christ, but we must pursue that holiness and develop and maintain it each day of our lives.[5] And the "indicative" aspect of our faith — who we are because of what Christ has done for us on the cross — provides us with sufficient motivation to become all that God has called us to be: his holy people.

Holiness and God's Discipline

It is for discipline that you have to endure. God is treating you as sons; for what son is there whom his father does not discipline? If you are left without discipline, in which all have participated, then you are illegitimate children and not sons. Besides this, we have had earthly fathers to discipline us and we respected them. Shall we not much more be subject to the Father of spirits and live? For they disciplined us for a short time at their pleasure, but he disciplines us for our good, *that we may share his holiness*. For the moment all discipline seems painful rather than pleasant; later it yields the peaceful fruit of righteousness to those who have been trained by it (Heb. 12:7-11).

Holiness doesn't come easily for any of us. Our sinful nature is so far from God's all-holy nature that considerable refinement is required. In ways which we may not realize, we are lacking in the holiness which God requires. This is where *discipline* comes in.

In Hebrews 12:3-11 the writer addresses his readers' situation of experiencing persecution. He describes this not as an unfortunate circumstance by which his readers were being victimized, but as "the discipline of the Lord." There is no indication in this paragraph that God was in some way "punishing" these Christians, or that he was angry with them.[6] Rather, "God is treating you as sons" (v. 7b). The author compares the discipline which we receive from our earthly fathers to that of our heavenly Father. The former disciplined us temporarily "at their pleasure," that is, as they saw fit, whether right or wrong. And many times, undoubtedly, they were wrong or unwise in their discipline. But God "disciplines us for our good, *that we may share his holiness*" (v. 10).[7] God's discipline, he says, "trains" us so that it yields in us "the peaceful fruit of righteousness" (v. 11). The readers are admonished to accept this discipline and to "strive for holiness" (vs. 12-15). God does not wish simply to forgive us; he has more in mind for us than that; he wants us to share his essential nature, to become like himself. "The end result in salvation is not that we should be left much as we were at the beginning but that we should be remade in the likeness of God."[8] This is what discipline is all about. But that discipline has to be accepted and God must be trusted as having a benevolent purpose, one which is entirely in our best interest.[9]

All discipline is the outgrowth of God's desire for us to share his holiness. It includes not only the discipline involved in sometimes facing persecution. It also includes disciplining *ourselves*. This is where "striving after holiness" comes in. We must decide that we want God's holiness and are willing to pursue it according to the teachings of his word. This will mean disciplining ourselves to worship, to pray, to serve, to study and live the word, to deny the tendencies of the flesh which war against those of the Spirit. We must accept the necessity of this aspect of God's discipline or else we will not be holy, and ultimately we will not "see the Lord."

Congregational discipline is likewise an extension of God's desire for our holiness. Just as God expects and requires us to discipline ourselves, he calls on us to discipline *each other* when necessary, not arbitrarily or angrily or vengefully, but as an outgrowth of his love and of his demand for holiness among his people. *It is no more "unloving" for us to discipline one another in the interest of holiness than it is for God to discipline us for the same purpose.* In fact, the lack of discipline is a distinctly un-God-like characteristic.

Although Hebrews does not explicitly connect holiness with *church* discipline,[10] the connection is strongly suggested in other New Testament texts. For example, in the notorious case of incest which had gone uncorrected at Corinth, Paul warns the church that "a little leaven leavens the whole lump" (I Cor. 5:6). Borrowing from Israel's Exodus/Passover experience, he warns the Corinthians that their holiness was threatened by the presence of undisciplined sin in their midst. And just as Israel had to remove the old leaven, so Paul admonishes the Corinthians to "Drive out the wicked person from among you" (v. 13). This formula occurs frequently in Deuteronomy following specific commands to the Israelites which were important for maintaining their holiness as the people of God. Likewise, in Matthew 18:17 Jesus commands that the "brother who sins" and cannot be persuaded to repent should "be to you as a Gentile and a tax collector." Both Gentiles and tax collectors were considered to have a defiling influence on righteous Jews and were thus to be avoided (Ex. 23:23-33, etc.; Lk. 15:1-2). So Jesus teaches that his holy followers must avoid unrepentant offenders in the interest of preserving their holiness. It is impossible to maintain holiness in the absence of discipline, both of ourselves and of others who insist on living unholy lives.

Holiness and Discipline Today

We have drifted far today from this concept of holiness and discipline, so far that many apparently believe that holiness can be maintained in the absence of discipline. It's not unusual, when someone begins to raise the subject of discipline, or when some disciplinary action is taken, to hear someone lament that this will surely cause trouble. Doesn't it say something about our lack of understanding of holiness that we label godly discipline as "trouble"? When there is unrepented sin in our midst, we already *have* trouble, and it will only get worse unless something is done to preserve or reinstate our holiness. John White and Ken Blue have written a stimulating book on church discipline as it relates to evangelicalism in general, and their comments on holiness apply no less to churches of Christ:

> Why is it that the thought of a holy and godly church concerns us so little? While the church of past centuries focused too much on purity to the exclusion of the other goals of corrective discipline, we have ignored it entirely too much. As stated earlier, we have become calloused to

sin. To our great shame, *holiness* has become an empty word. Can it be because we have other goals for the church, goals which supersede her holiness? Does our preoccupation with building programs, with our public image in the community, with our innovative programming or with our church growth suffocate our concern for the holiness of God's people?

We are blind. As churches we no longer see God. Only the pure in heart see him and our hearts are no longer pure. We even forget that we are at war. The hosts of wickedness are doing all they can to befoul the bride of Jesus. How better could they express their hatred of him? If you are honest you will admit that at times it is hard to conceive the ferocity and the intensity of the battles in heavenly places, the heinous and implacable will of evil to destroy and to mar anything that bears the name of Jesus. And so we play church while the fires of hell rage round us. What ought we to be doing? We ought to be exercising corrective church discipline. It is a matter of life and death for the church.[11]

In our era of incredibly lax moral standards, there is a temptation for the church to neglect discipline in the interests of maintaining "relevance" to the world around us. After all, when the rest of the world (including many churches) is condoning everything from same-sex marriages to abortion, won't we seem more than a little out of touch if we censure people's conduct and even put some out of the church? Aren't we only hurting ourselves and the cause of Christ by doing something that is so bizarre and outdated? But it is precisely *because* of the horrendous moral and spiritual climate in which we live that discipline is more essential than ever before! The secular influences of immorality, materialism, and self-centeredness threaten to invade the church — and are invading it — to an unparalleled degree. In the predominately "Christian society" in which many of us grew up, the church could refrain from discipline without much immediate effect. After all, our standards were, in many places at least, basically the same as most of society around us. But we no longer have the luxury of allowing sin to go uncorrected in our midst — if, indeed, we ever had it. Now discipline is a matter of survival. If we do not resist the ungodly influences of the world through discipline, the world will transform us into its own image, rather than our being transformed into the likeness of Christ.

God disciplines us "that we may share his holiness," and without his holiness, "no one will see the Lord." Dare we refuse to discipline? Dare we allow ourselves to be comfortable in our disobedience?

1. Rudolf Otto, *The Idea of the Holy,* translated by John W. Harvey (New York: Oxford University Press, 1958 edition) 24ff.

2. The adjective *hagios* ("holy") and related terms occurs twenty-six times in Hebrews. It is derived from the old Greek term *hagos* which denotes an object of awe. The adjective *hages* means "clean," and the verb *hazo* has the sense "to shrink from." *Hagios* is used of sanctuaries ("holy places") and later of gods and religious practices. In the NT, holiness expresses God's innermost nature and embraces omnipotence, eternity, and glory, and evokes awe. See D. Proksch and O. Proksch, "*hagios,* etc." in *Theological Dictionary of the New Testament*, ed. by G. Kittel and G. Friedrich; abridged in one volume by G. W. Bromiley (Grand Rapids: Eerdmans, 1985) 14-16.

3. *Christian Holiness* (London: Lutterworth, 1960) 110.

4. In Classical Greek *hosios* denotes what is in accordance with divine direction and providence or is sanctioned or hallowed by divine or natural law. "The use of *hosios* in Heb. 7:26 is unique. Here the word is used absolutely in the way in which elsewhere it can be used only of God. As high priest Christ is *hosios*, utterly without sin and utterly pure, so that his offering is sufficient once and for all" (H. Seebass, *The New International Dictionary of New Testament Theology*, Vol. 2, ed. by Colin Brown [Grand Rapids: Zondervan, 1976] 236-38).

5. "Holiness is a state into which we have been brought by the offering of the body of Jesus once for all; but it is realized only in a constantly renewed obedience to the One who was himself obedient . . . Christian holiness, whether for the Church or for the individual, can never be a static thing, something gained once for all. It has to be maintained amid conflicts and

      perils that are renewed day by day. It is a moving thing; it can only exist as a function of pilgrimage" (Neill, 111-12).

6.   The presence of the words "punishes" and "chastises" in vs. 5-6 does not necessarily indicate that the original readers of Hebrews were being punished. Rather, these terms are part of the quotation from Proverbs 3:11-12, which the author cites because it teaches the principle that those disciplined by God (even if they *are* being punished) are loved by him.

7.   "Earthly discipline confines itself to the sphere of earthly life; but heavenly discipline, which is never arbitrary, seeks to purge God's own from sin and secure for them a permanent participation in the divine life whose essential requirement is holiness" (Neil R. Lightfoot, *Jesus Christ Today: A Commentary on the Book of Hebrews* [Grand Rapids: Baker, 1976] 233. Now reprinted in paperback [Bible Guides, P. O. Box 273, Abilene, TX 79604]).

8.   Leon Morris, *Bible Study Commentary: Hebrews* (Grand Rapids: Zondervan, 1983) 123.

9.   "The clear implication of verse 10 is that it is impossible to share in God's holiness apart from the correction administered through disciplinary sufferings, which have the effect of maturing us as men and women of God" (William L. Lane, *Call to Commitment* [Nashville: Thomas Nelson, 1985] 164).

10.   The connection is made implicitly in 12:15: "See to it (*episkopeo*) that no one fail to obtain the grace of God. . . ." *Episkopeo* is a verb which denotes watching out for or oversight. It is related to the noun *episkopos*, which is usually translated as "bishop," or "overseer." The concept of mutuality is evident in this verse.

11.   John White and Ken Blue, *Healing the Wounded: The Costly Love of Church Discipline* (Downers Grove, Ill.: InterVarsity, 1985) 59.

FOR THOUGHT AND DISCUSSION

1. If someone were to ask, "Are you holy?", how would you probably respond? Why?

2. What images does the word "holiness" bring to your mind? Positive? Negative?

3. In what sense is holiness something which we already have, and yet something toward which we must strive? Give some concrete examples of both kinds of holiness in the life of the Christian.

4. What kind of discussions (sermons, Bible classes, etc.) about holiness have you heard in the church? Were they helpful or not? Why?

5. Explain in your own words the connection between discipline and sharing the holiness of God.

"Even if it may not be this week's fad in American theology, something of the nature of church discipline has always been part of the life of the people of God."
— Marlin Jeschke, *Discipling in the Church*

NO DISCIPLINE, NO CHURCH[1]

Everyone at the West Side church was shocked at the unbelievable news that one of their most beloved and active members had left his wife of over twenty years for another woman. Ron had been a Bible class teacher, an effective personal evangelist, a fellowship group leader, as well as a seemingly model husband and father. His adultery had a strangely numbing effect on the congregation: no one even wanted to talk about what had happened, and nothing was even said—at least not openly—about disciplining him. Ron was just there one day, and gone the next! But in spite of his sin, Ron's faith meant too much to him to be forgotten, and he missed his active role in the church. So a few years later he re-surfaced, this time at another congregation across town, bringing his new wife with him and asking to be accepted as a member, but with no indication of repentance. Meanwhile, members from West Side would occasionally encounter Ron socially. At first it was uncomfortable, but Ron didn't act as if anything was wrong, and soon the discomfort left for most people. But for several there were serious questions about how they should regard him, or even if they should associate with him at all. After all, he was an adulterer. But then, he hadn't been disciplined. . . .

This fictionalized but oft-repeated story raises some difficult dilemmas. Exactly what is Ron's standing with the church? Since he was never disciplined at West Side nor made any move to withdraw his membership there, is he still a member? And, since he was not disciplined where he was a member, what should the leadership of the second congregation do about him, assuming that they know about his questionable marriage and spiritual status? Can he be a member there, or must he return to West Side and "make things right" there? If the second congregation refuses to grant him membership, on what grounds may they do so? What if he leaves that church and moves away and becomes identified with a church that knows nothing of him or his past? And what is the status of a church that becomes filled with "Rons"? Does God still recognize it as his church? If not, at what point does it cease to be so? And what of Ron's friends at his old congregation? Do they continue to be friendly with Ron as if nothing had ever happened, in hopes that he will someday "come to his senses"? Or should they exercise a personal responsibility to avoid him, even though the congregation as a whole has not responded to his sin?

At this point we are talking about a function of church discipline known among social scientists as "boundary maintenance." Any group, religious or otherwise, which claims unique status must have and maintain clearly-demarcated boundaries, so that it can be seen by all who is and is not in the group. And if boundaries are to be maintained, there must be some process by which members who violate the norms of the group (i. e., put themselves outside the group boundaries) can be identified and/or removed. Otherwise the group eventually loses its identity. The church of Christ is no exception to this. In fact, it is uniquely true of the church, since we claim to be the people of God, and since the Bible gives us the guidelines by which God's people are called to live. We must recognize the inescapable conclusion that discipline is a necessary corollary to the nature of the church as it is described in the Bible: "No discipline, no church." Not that this loss of identity happens at a given moment in time, or that it can be discerned by the human eye. But the second and third chapters of Revelation make it clear that at some point God will "remove the lampstand" from those churches which violate his will and refuse to repent. And they may not even know it! This does not happen because we fail to maintain discipline as an "identifying mark of the church," and thereby disqualify ourselves as a New Testament church.[2] (If this is true, there are a lot fewer "true churches" than most of us think!) It happens, rather, because the lack of discipline violates the very nature of the church itself. K. Brynhof Lyon describes this process as he sees it at work among the Disciples of Christ:

> Through a systematic misunderstanding of our history, Disciples' congregations have often seemed to many persons to be fertile soil for individualistic (really subjectivistic) understandings of the Christian life. At its extreme, this suggests that discipline in almost any sense is nonsense since church members can believe anything they want to believe about what constitutes a fitting enactment of the Christian witness. Yet, clearly, when this becomes the church's "norm" of congregational life, it tends to suggest that the church stands for nothing precisely because it stands for anything.[3]

If we are going to restore the God-intended role of discipline in the church today, we must restore the New Testament understanding of the nature of the church. Once we have done this, it will be obvious to any thinking observer that discipline must follow, in order to maintain the identity which Scripture says we have as followers of Jesus Christ.

The Church as the Unique Body of Christ

The New Testament makes it clear that the early Christians accepted the convictions of Judaism that "God is one" and added that there is "one Lord Jesus Christ" (I Cor. 8:6). As a corollary to this, Paul emphasizes that there is but "one body, the church" (Eph. 1:22-23, 4:4ff; I Cor. 12:12-13). All others "do not know God" (I Thess. 4:5, Gal. 4:8-9). The social expression of this monotheism is the exclusive unity of the worshipers. This accounts for what one writer has called "the language of belonging" and "the language of separation" which occurs so frequently in Paul's letters.[4] For example, church members are called "saints" (holy ones, set apart ones—I Cor. 1:2, II Cor. 1:1, Phil. 1:1) and the "elect" (I Thess. 1:4, Rom. 8:33, I Cor. 1:27). This is "the language of belonging." "The language of separation" includes such terms for non-members as "the outsiders" (I Cor. 5:12-13, I Thess. 4:12) "non-believers, " "the unrighteous, " and "those despised in the church" (I Cor. 6:1, 4, 9); and "those who do not know God" (I Thess. 4:5, Gal. 4:8).[5] In addition, there is Paul's "body" analogy which he uses to express the special unity-in-diversity that characterizes community members (Rom. 12:4-5, I Cor. 12:12-26).

With this understanding of the nature of the church in mind, the necessity for discipline becomes obvious. The boundary between the church and the world must be maintained, and discipline is one of the God-ordained ways of doing so.

Baptism and the Lord's Supper have a special role in reinforcing the concept of boundary establishment and maintenance. Baptism is the "rite of initiation" by which one becomes a part of the church, so it is relatively clear who is "in" and who is "out" (Rom. 6:3-5; I Cor. 1:16-17, 12:13; Gal. 3:26-27).[6] Being put out of the church's fellowship, then, might be viewed as the reverse of baptism, although there is no suggestion in Scripture that restored penitents must be "re-baptized." Similarly, the Lord's Supper is an act of solidarity for the church, as are more common "fellowship meals." Being barred from participation in these, especially the Lord's Supper, takes on deep significance, and it is not surprising that in Paul's letters we find references to such disciplinary practices. For example, Paul says that we are "not even to eat" with a "so-called brother" who is sexually immoral, greedy, idolatrous, or is a slanderer, drunkard, or swindler (I Cor. 5:11). Although scholars point out that it is unclear whether the prohibition against eating with an offending brother means ordinary meals in general or the Lord's Supper in particular, it seems logical to think that Paul meant both. How could one have any disciplinary effect without the other? Besides, while the offender may make the decision himself/herself whether to assemble with the church for communion, it is our decision whether to meet for lunch! How can we do either with someone who has flouted the norms of the Christian life, without reinforcing such conduct and compromising the church's solidarity? Likewise, Paul reminds the Thessalonian church of a rule which he had left them when they were first evangelized: "If a man will not work, he shall not eat" (II Thess. 3:10). This is probably a reference to the church's sharing its common store of food (the "pantry") with those of its number who refuse to support themselves. But in both instances Paul makes it clear that sharing food is a sign of fellowship, and being banned from such meals is an overt act of discipline.

The Church as a Family

Closely tied to the concept of the church as the exclusive body of Christ is the concept of the church as family. This arises obviously from the Biblical conception of God as "Father" and believers as his "children." Also, since local communities usually met in members' homes, the family becomes a quite natural model for the Christian community, which is reinforced by the language of family ("brother — Rom. 8:29, 16:33; I Cor. 1:1, 5:11, 16:12; II Cor. 1:1; Phil. 2:25; "sister"—Rom. 16:1; I Cor. 7:15, 9:5; Philem. 2)

Such a concept of family unity and loyalty implies the need for discipline. Just as we can see the quite visible effects of a lack of parental discipline within a family we can see it in numerous congregations of the Lord's people, if we will only open our eyes and acknowledge the real problem. Likewise, what the Bible says about avoiding, excluding from fellowship, warning, and admonishing is understandable only in the context of a high degree of cohesion within the body. Where such unity and family identity exists, being disciplined by the group has serious implications for one's sense of belonging and social stability.

The Church as Those Destined to Receive Eternal Life

The heart of our faith is, of course, the conviction that Jesus was crucified for our sins and then rose from the dead. This leads to the conviction that those who follow Christ can also expect to be raised from the dead (I Cor. 15, I Thess. 4:13-18). Conversely, those outside the body are destined for condemnation (Rom. 2:6-8, 8:6-7; I Cor. 6:9-11, 15:12-19; Gal. 6:7-10). Discipline follows inevitably from such a concept. Those within the church must be influenced not to abandon their hope, and the boundary between those headed for salvation and those destined for destruction must be kept sharply distinct, at least to the extent that such distinctions can be made by us. This might seem intimidating, but we should remember such Biblical declarations as "By their fruits you shall know them, " and "The works of the flesh are obvious."

When the Boundaries Become Blurred

Without consistent, lovingly-applied congregational discipline, it becomes impossible to maintain the boundaries between church and world. Members like Ron come and go, undisciplined, unredeemed, unreclaimed. Confusion reigns, as suggested in Ron's story. Does the church take a stand against sin, or does it not? Is there really any difference between "us" and the rest of the world, or is that only a pious figment of our imaginations, held over from the past?

And can we truly call people out of the world through the gospel, when the world is so much with us?

And, can we legitimately claim to be the Lord's people when we steadfastly refuse to discipline ourselves and each other, as his Word so clearly teaches? At what point does he "move the lampstand"?

1. The title of this chapter is borrowed from the title of an article by Kenneth R. Davis, "No Discipline, No Church: An Anabaptist Contribution to the Reformed Tradition," *Sixteenth Century Journal* XIII No. 4 (1982) 43-58.

2. This was the position of the Protestant Reformers, and has been the position of many within churches of Christ as well.

3. "The Discipline of Congregational Life: Prospects and Resources for Renewal," *Midstream* Vol. 26 (July, 1987) 403. Lyon proposes a renewal of congregational discipline as a necessary corrective to this situation. In this same issue, see C. Leonard Allen, "Congregational Life and Discipline: An Historical Perspective, " 379-90, who discusses the historical tension between the church and the world and the role of discipline in maintaining the distinction.

4. Wayne Meeks, *The First Urban Christians: The Social World of the Apostle Paul* (New Haven: Yale University Press, 1983) 85 and 94.

5. "Repetitive use of such special terms for the group and its members plays a role in the process of re-socialization by which an individual's identity is revised and knit together with the identity of the group, especially when it is accompanied by special terms also for 'the outsiders, ' 'the world.' By this kind of talk members are taught to conceive of only two classes of humanity: the sect and outsiders" (Meeks, 86). It should be noted that "sect" is Meeks' term for any group which sees itself as distinct from all others.

6. Most congregations of the church today make some sort of distinction in their membership directories between the baptized and the unbaptized even in the same family, even when both attend and otherwise participate regularly. Likewise, most congregations refuse to allow the unbaptized to lead in worship, teach publicly, etc.

FOR THOUGHT AND DISCUSSION

1. Has there ever been someone like Ron in the congregation where you worship? How was the situation handled? What difficulties did it create?

2. Explain the relationship between baptism and the Lord's Supper and "boundary maintenance" within the church.

3. Does the church today make much use of "insider/outsider" language? Why or why not?

4. What is the effect on congregations when the boundaries between who is "in" and who isn't become blurred?

5. What impact does the blurring of boundaries have on the world's attitude toward the church?

"The more bitter the truth, the better the friend who tells it."
— Sir Pellinore to King Arthur, *Camelot*

THE ULTIMATE EXPRESSION
OF FELLOWSHIP

Dr. Flavil Yeakley, Jr. tells of a meeting between the elders and deacons of a church, at which the elders announced that they were about to "withdraw fellowship"[1] from several families who had not attended worship in months, some even in years. Following their announcement, one of the deacons asked, "What will they miss once fellowship is withdrawn?" The elders at first didn't understand the question, but the deacon went on to explain that a "withdrawal of fellowship" could have little meaning or effect if there were no fellowship to withdraw. It seems that if fellowship is withdrawn, those so disciplined should find themselves *missing* something. The elders met to consider this point, and at a later meeting with the deacons, announced that they were about to begin an effort toward intensive *fellowship* with those same couples from whom they had been about to withdraw. For several weeks the elders visited these people in their homes, hosted them in their own homes for meals, and generally spent time getting acquainted with them and discussing their spiritual needs. In a few months' time most of these people had acknowledged their negligence and recommitted themselves to the Lord.

This true story highlights two of the most overlooked

aspects of corrective discipline: (1) it is utterly without meaning outside the context of genuine congregational fellowship, and (2) the exercise of discipline is, in fact, the ultimate expression of fellowship. It is the *most* that we can do to maintain fellowship with a brother or sister who has been overtaken by sin.

Fellowship Before Discipline

One thing wrong with the scenario presented in the Introduction is the practice of "withdrawing fellowship" from members whom no one in the church really even knows any more. Any time a church has to search for its members in order to "discipline" them, something is seriously wrong with that church's fellowship and with its leadership. Outside the context of fellowship, discipline can only be destructive, and that is certainly not its intent in Scripture. In Matthew 18 Jesus instructs disciples to carry out disciplinary measures in order to "gain your brother." Galatians 6:1 teaches "the spiritual" not to "get rid of" an offending brother, but to "restore" him. "Brother" is a fellowship word, and it is almost always used in the New Testament when discipline is the topic of discussion.[2] A notable exception is texts which deal with those whose divisiveness and/or heresy is so severe that they are simply to be avoided (cf. Rom. 16:17, Tit. 3:10-11; contrast II Thess. 3:6, 14-15). But other than in these situations, the assumption is always that "the offender" is someone in our midst, not a name on a list compiled years ago![3]

It has sometimes been observed that many cases of congregational discipline are meaningless because, as we have indicated above, there is "nothing to withdraw" (that is, any real fellowship). The situation is actually much worse than that! Apart from fellowship, discipline is not only meaningless, it is abusive. To discipline someone with whom we have not enjoyed real fellowship is much like spanking a stranger's child. We have no relationship with that child; therefore discipline is traumatic and inexplicable. No wonder that so many cases of "withdrawing fellowship" are entirely ineffective and leave a bad taste in the mouths of the entire congregation! Where there is no fellowship, there is no valid context for carrying out discipline. One of the first lessons to be learned about discipline is that you cannot discipline someone you don't really care about. The truth is that most congregations cannot effectively discipline their members, because there isn't sufficient fellowship to make such actions meaningful.

> Christian fellowship is to restore what human society has lost through sin. But has it done so? Warmer, deeper fellowships exist among Christians. But they are not common. Who feels safe enough in the average church to open up to fellow Christians, to share the painful, shameful and even the trivial everyday things that community was meant to be all about? How would our confidences be received? With polite boredom? Dismay? Gossip? Instead we hide behind our social masks, enjoying what we can, but never being off our guard. A sociologist studying the average Christian church would see no essential difference in the quality of its human relationships and those of some local club, say a community service group or a country club.[4]

Discipline as an Expression of Fellowship

But not only is fellowship the appropriate and necessary context for discipline, disciplinary acts are themselves an extension of our fellowship. We discipline *because* we are in fellowship — not because we no longer desire to be. If our fellowship is real, we cannot simply sit by and watch a brother or sister become entangled in sin and do nothing to reclaim them. What kind of "fellowship" is it when we see the devastating effects of sin in the life of another Christian, yet refuse to openly and lovingly express our concern? Even the most extreme form of discipline, the withdrawal of fellowship, is an expression of fellowship — the ultimate expression of fellowship. It says to the disciplined persons that they are simply too important for us to lose them to Satan without doing everything within our power to reclaim them, and that we would rather be deprived of our association with them for a time now than to be without them for all eternity. It is not by accident that Jesus' disciplinary instructions in Matthew 18 come in context immediately after the paragraph about the lost sheep (see Chapters 5 and 6). It is not God's will for any of his people to perish, so every brother or sister who strays is to be reclaimed at all cost — even the cost of association with those we love dearly.[5]

When real fellowship exists, we will more readily "go to" our brothers and sisters as Jesus taught us to do in a spirit of loving concern. Cases of withdrawal will be rare, because most problems will be addressed before they get to that point. On the other hand, where no real fellowship exists, there will be no discipline, or else only "formal" disciplinary acts will occur, and they will be consistently ineffective.

Fellowship is the reason (communally speaking) for discipline to occur, and it is what gives it its impact: the fear of being disapproved by or possibly even losing contact with those with whom we have served and praised our Lord. These are difficult pressures to bring to bear on a loved one, but there are times when genuine love requires it.

A common objection to the practice of discipline is that it will only embitter those who are disciplined, and, as a result, make matters worse. Naturally there are no guarantees that such measures will be effective, but if our fellowship is genuine, we must try, if we truly believe that those who go into sin and away from Christ have lost their fellowship with the Lord.

> While it is true that offenders ejected from the local congregation may become embittered and plunge further into sin, it is also true that others discover the disenchantment and miseries of sin. These in turn can awaken a hunger for true spiritual consolation and

fellowship, especially if the offender left a church flaming with true koinonia, warmed by a faithful, loving Christian fellowship. Cold is never so cold as when you begin to recall the fires of home.[6]

What I have been describing is, of course, a somewhat idealized concept of congregational fellowship. Even within churches where genuine fellowship exists, there are always "levels" of fellowship. Some members remain "on the fringes" by choice or due to lack of commitment or understanding of the meaning of discipleship. Others are new in the church and haven't yet been fully assimilated. Does this mean that discipline cannot be undertaken until an ideal state of fellowship is attained? Or does it suggest that those "on the fringes" shouldn't be subjected to congregational discipline?

The answer to both questions is certainly "No." The churches about which we read in the New Testament were not perfect, either in fellowship or in other aspects of congregational life. And discipline may sometimes be needed to bring those "on the fringes" closer to the center of God's will, or to prevent their leaving the church entirely. What is essential here is not the perfection of our fellowship, but the recognition that we must be striving continually for a more perfect fellowship, and that only when we care about one another can discipline do what God intends it to do.

My suggestion to any eldership, preacher, member, or congregation who is concerned about disciplining according to the Scriptures, is to begin by striving to create an environment of love and fellowship, "a church flaming with true koinonia." Rather than beginning with a list of names out of the past, begin with the people you now have and with whom you are in weekly contact. Disciplinary acts in the present cannot erase our fellowship failures of the past. Promote genuine participation in one another's lives, true pastoral concern on the part of elders, real service to one another, the teaching of truth in love, and a spirit of concern for each other in good times and in bad — including when sin arises. *We must promote "intensive fellowship" before even thinking about intensive discipline.*

Rather than simply recognizing our lack of discipline, we must see the larger problem: lack of fellowship. If we work to correct the more basic problem, then effective, godly discipline can occur in our churches.

1. Although it is not a Biblical term, this is the expression most often used in churches of Christ for excluding someone from fellowship. Catholics (and others) employ the term "excommunication," which means essentially the same thing. The New Testament terminology varies considerably by using general terms for avoidance. (See the appropriate later chapters.) There is no "technical" term used consistently in the NT for this practice.

2. The New Revised Standard Version obscures this point in the interest of inclusive language by rendering *adelphos* by such terms as "another member of the church," "this one," "the offender," etc.

3. On the relationship between fellowship and discipline, see Jimmy Jividen, *Koinonia: A Place of Tough and Tender Love* (Nashville: Gospel Advocate, 1989) Section 4, 145-94.

4. White and Blue, 55.

5. Lest we think that the joy of fellowship and the sorrow of discipline are somehow incompatible, Paul reminds us that in the context of genuine fellowship, we should "Rejoice with those who rejoice" and "weep with those who weep" (Rom. 12:15).

6. White and Blue, 106.

FOR THOUGHT AND DISCUSSION

1. Have you ever personally witnessed situations where discipline was administered apart from fellowship? What was the outcome?

2. On a scale of one to ten, how would you rate the level of spiritual fellowship in the congregation where you worship? Compare your response to that of others.

3. In what sense does discipline express fellowship? Why can there be no true fellowship if there is no willingness to discipline one another?

4. What could your congregation do to improve the level and quality of its fellowship? What could you do personally?

5. Why do you think churches of Christ have generally avoided the term "excommunication" in favor of the term "disfellowship"?

"Truth is not only violated by falsehood; it may be equally outraged by silence."

— Henri Amiel

SPEAKING THE TRUTH IN LOVE

Ephesians 4 is Paul's well-known appeal for the church to "maintain the unity of the Spirit in the bond of peace." He has already demonstrated in previous chapters that the unity of the church is built-in by God, that the "mystery," the plan of God from before the foundation of the world, is that all humanity should be united in one body, the church. Therefore, the church is not called upon to *create* unity; God has already done that. Our task is simply to *maintain* it — that is, to do all that we can to promote it and not do anything to destroy it! This is the only way that we can "live a life worthy of the calling we have received" (v. 1).

As a basis for his appeal, Paul reminds us of the essentials of faith which make us one in Christ: one body, one Spirit, one hope, one Lord, one faith, one baptism, one God (vs. 4-6). Yet within that unity there is a marvelous diversity of "gifts" that enable people of various talents and strengths to function as a unit for the good of the whole and to the glory of God. So Paul reminds us of this diversity in verses 5-14.

Then, in verses 15-16, Paul challenges us to maintain a balance in our church life which is extremely difficult for Christians to achieve — the balance between truth and love:

Rather, speaking the truth in love, we are to grow up in

every way into him who is the head, into Christ, from whom the whole body, joined and knit together by every joint with which it is supplied, when each part is working properly, makes bodily growth and upbuilds itself in love.

As we all know too well, it is easy to speak the truth without love. But such truthfulness can be brutal and destructive. On the other hand, there are people who believe that they can love others without telling them the truth, but such "love" is an illusion, a mere sappy sentimentality. But when Christians practice "speaking the truth in love," Paul says that wonderful results occur: the church is spiritually healthier, we grow into the likeness of Christ, who is the embodiment of truth in love, and we move on to maturity and growth. Perhaps this explains why so many churches never attain the kind of church life which Paul describes, why, in spite of all the techniques of "church growth," most churches don't. Maybe our problem is, in part, at least, an absence of the practice of "truth in love." And, as we will see, what we call "church discipline" has a vital role to play in maintaining the balance between truth and love.

What Is "Truth"?

But first we need to ask, "What kind of 'truth' is Paul talking about?" The usual understanding of this text is that Paul is calling for a mutual confession of the same *doctrinal* truth. This fits well in the context, since in verse 14 he has said that we need to get past the stage of being "tossed to and fro and carried about with every wind of doctrine." And speaking the truth in love has a lot to do with this. This is consistent with Paul's own practice in his ministry, since he proclaims that "We have renounced disgraceful, underhanded ways; we refuse to practice cunning or to tamper with God's word, but by the open statement of the truth we would commend ourselves to every man's conscience in the sight of God" (II Cor. 4:2). This "truth" Paul proclaimed so openly was obviously the gospel. A common commitment to doctrinal truth is essential to the maintenance of unity and fellowship. But this open statement of doctrinal truth must be done lovingly, not, as is sometimes done, without regard to the impact of truth on people. Even "hard" truths can be said lovingly.

But it seems unlikely that doctrinal truth is all that Paul has in mind in these verses. A common adherence to specific doctrines will not by itself effect the kind of unity he describes. There is a corresponding need for what we might call *"personal"* truth. The word which most English translations render as "speaking the truth" (*aletheuo*) doesn't necessarily refer to speaking. Truth is more than mere "verbal accuracy," and this word includes both "speaking the truth" and "dealing truly, "[1] "being utterly genuine, sincere, and honest."[2] This understanding likewise fits well in the context of Ephesians 4:15, since in the previous verse Paul has mentioned cunning, craftiness, and deceit. Christians, by contrast, are to be genuine, truthful people. In today's language, Paul is saying that we need to "be real" with each other, both in our speech and actions.

Several verses later, in 4:25, personal truth is clearly Paul's concern. "Therefore, putting away falsehood, let every one speak the truth with his neighbor, for we are members one of another." Notice that here the motive for being truthful with one another is our *fellowship*. Being untruthful with each other is the surest way to destroy or prevent fellowship. People who will not "be real" with each other can never enjoy real spiritual unity. Being untruthful is one of the most *un*-Christian things we can do. According to Colossians 3:9-10, it is part of the "old life" which should have been put away at conversion: "Do not lie to one another, seeing that you have put off the old nature with its practices and have put on the new nature, which is being renewed in knowledge after the image of its creator." Being untruthful with one another is simply not in harmony with the image of God, the image into which we are supposed to be transformed.

Being Truthful About Ourselves and Others

Taking the discussion a step further, there are two aspects of personal truth/"being real" which are essential to fellowship. The first is being individually truthful *about ourselves*. We must be willing to confess our own neediness, our struggles, our problems — even our sins. We are not called together as the body of Christ because we are paragons of righteousness, not because we are "okay" and need to serve as examples for others to strive after. We are called together in Christ because in and of ourselves we *aren't* "okay." And because we aren't, we need the Lord and each other. But in most congregations, such honesty about self seldom occurs. Few of us want to allow ourselves to be seen as we really are. What would people think, if they knew the truth about my marriage? my children? my temptations? my frustrations? my doubts? my fears? And so we hide our real selves, and then wonder why we feel so empty, so alone, even in the midst of the family of God! This is tragic, because the very truthfulness we so studiously avoid has the power to set us free. When the woman with the flow of blood touched the hem of Jesus' garment, she did so secretly, because she knew she was unclean and that her action was socially and religiously unacceptable. But when Jesus asked who it was who touched him, she "came in fear and trembling and fell down before him, and *told him the whole truth*" (Mark 5:33). As a result, Jesus told her to "be healed" of her infirmity. In the same way, a great deal of healing can take place in our lives when we are willing to be honest about ourselves in the presence of our brothers and sisters in Christ.

The other aspect of personal truth that we urgently need in our churches is truthfulness *about each other*. There are times when we need to confront each other lovingly about our actions and attitudes, to help each other see the reality of what is going on in our lives. Jesus taught that "If your brother sins, go and tell him his fault between you and him alone" (Matt. 18:15). But it doesn't happen very often in most churches, does it? As a result, much fellowship is broken (or, never develops) because of offenses, misunderstandings, and miscommunications that could have been resolved simply by "being real" with each other. When Jesus taught us to go to our offending brother, it was simply another way of saying, "Speak the truth in love."

The Risk of Truthfulness

We tend to find such truth-telling difficult, but it's no less necessary. The reason we find it so hard is *fear*. I may fear what others will think of me if they know the truth about me. Will I find understanding and help? Or will I become the object of gossip? All of us rightly fear alienating or offending others if we approach them about problems in their lives, no matter how lovingly we may do so. Some people simply do not want to hear the truth and will take offense. Paul knew that risk. After scolding the Galatian churches for abandoning their trust in Christ in favor of legalism, he asks, "Have I now become your enemy by telling you the truth?" (Gal. 4:16). There is an old Yugoslav proverb which says, "Tell the truth — and run!"

Part of our fear may be of "causing trouble" within the congregation where we worship. No one wants to be the source of trouble, but we often forget that *sin* is the worst form of trouble we can have — not honesty about sin. Jesus once proclaimed that his enemies wanted to kill him precisely because he had told them the truth about themselves (Jn. 8:45). Truth-telling can be risky business, but the reality is that love is *always* risky. When we speak truthfully with someone, we run the risk of being rejected or even recriminated aqainst, so it is easier to keep silent.

Yet over and over again the Scriptures teach us to speak the truth. When Jesus encountered the Samaritan woman at the well (Jn. 4), he did not allow her to avoid the truth about her spiritual condition, based on her sad marital history. His goal in probing about her marriages was not to embarrass her or to cause pain, but she had to face the truth: she desperately needed the "living water." And he had to confront her with the truth in order to get her to realize it.

Paul instructs the Thessalonians to "respect those who labor among you and are over you in the Lord and admonish you" (I Thess. 5:12); likewise, two verses later he exhorts them to "admonish the idlers, encourage the fainthearted, help the weak, be patient with them all." To "admonish" someone means to warn, advise, remind, teach, and spur them on to better conduct.[3] Far from being an exceptional activity within the life of the church, Paul indicates that it should be the norm. In encouraging Timothy in fulfilling his ministry, Paul charges him to "convince, rebuke, and exhort" (II Tim. 4:2). Likewise he tells Titus to "rebuke. . . sharply" the Cretan false teachers and to admonish only "once or twice" the divisive man before avoiding him completely (Tit. 1:13, 3:10-11). Even elders who "persist in sin" are to be rebuked "in the presence of all" (I Tim. 5:20).

In other words, we are all subject to such failings, but that doesn't mean that they are to be ignored when we see them gaining a foothold in one another's lives. Rather, they are to be confronted truthfully and lovingly so that the necessary corrections can be made. This, too, is a form of "discipline," one which, if practiced more consistently than is usually the case, would prevent many bad situations from becoming worse. Where the truth is regularly spoken in love, discipline will occur naturally and spontaneously. For speaking the truth in love *is* discipline, or at least the beginnings of it.

Truthfulness vs. Pretense

The opposite of this kind of truth-telling is not lying, but *pretense*. When we are not truthful with each other, then we pretend that all is well, even though we know that it isn't. And *nothing* is more damaging to real fellowship than pretense. Pretending that I'm okay, even though deep inside I am hurting and needing help. Pretending that there is no sin in my brother or sister's life when it's obvious to all that there is. Pretending that someone's ugly, divisive attitude isn't doing harm to the body of Christ. Pretending to be friends with people whom we really resent because of offenses or misunderstandings never resolved. Where such practices exist, real fellowship cannot! And to speak of "fellowship" without truth-telling makes a sham out of the concept.

"Speaking the truth in love." "Put away falsehood." "Let us speak the truth with our neighbor, for we are members one of another." In all of these ways, the Bible is telling us to "be real" with each other. By openly declaring the gospel truths which make us one body in Christ. By confessing our own weaknesses and struggles and sins and thereby our need for Christ and each other. By lovingly confronting each other about our sins when necessary. Only when we speak the truth in love will we see the church "grow up in every way into him who is the head, into Christ" and "make bodily growth and upbuild itself in love."

1. Francis Foulkes, *The Epistle of Paul to the Ephesians* (Grand Rapids: Eerdmans, 1963) 123.

2. C. L. Mitton, *New Century Bible Commentary: Ephesians* (Grand Rapids: Eerdmans, 1973) 156.

3. F. Selter, "Exhort, etc.," *The New International Dictionary of New Testament Theology*, Vol. 1 (Grand Rapids: Zondervan, 1975) 567.

FOR THOUGHT AND DISCUSSION

1.   What happens when the truth is spoken without love? What happens when there is "love" (emotionally) but no speaking of the truth?   '

2.   What are some ways in which Christians sometimes fail to deal truthfully with one another?

3.   Why do you think we are so often reluctant to "be real" with one another? What can we (you) do to correct this situation?

4.   How can truth-telling sometimes be risky business? Give some specific examples.

5.   Explain in your own words why pretense is damaging to fellowship.

"A disciplining church will prove more loving in the long run than a church that advertises God's love but then shows no interest in whether this love is practiced by her members. . . . A church that disciples people into an undisciplined church lives a lie. Integrity requires both inner and outer mission."

— F. D. Bruner, Matthew, Volume 2

I *AM* MY BROTHER'S KEEPER

(MATTHEW 18:15-17)

When God questioned Cain concerning the whereabouts of his murdered brother, he responded defiantly, "I do not know; am I my brother's keeper?" (Gen. 4:9).

Although Cain's motive was evil, his question was good, and is one that we ought to ask as well: *"Am* I my brother's keeper?" To what extent am I responsible for you and you for me, and for the person who sits next to both of us on the pew each Sunday morning?

The answer in Genesis 4 was a resounding "Yes!" Cain *was* responsible for what happened to his brother — and so are we, even more so in the kingdom of God. Because we are God's children and brothers and sisters to one another, we are our "brother's keeper" — not in any manipulative sense, as practiced in the "discipling" churches, where people "ride herd" on one another's spirituality (and lives in general). But there is a legitimate sphere of spiritual responsibility for one another's welfare, and that is Jesus' concern in Matthew 18:15-17. In this chapter and the next we'll take a closer look at this important text in order to see what that responsibility entails.

Matthew 18:15-17 in Context

It is impossible to over-estimate the importance of this text for the study of godly church discipline. It is the most comprehensive of all New Testament texts on the subject, since it covers the "big picture" from offense to loving confrontation to withdrawal and forgiveness. Likewise, it is, along with Galatians 6:1, the most general text on discipline, because it discusses "sins" in general rather than specific cases of sin. And since it contains the explicit teachings of Jesus himself on the subject and serves as the foundational principle for later New Testament statements[1] about discipline, it is important that we understand thoroughly what is being said here. To do this, we must begin with a good grasp of the context in which these words were spoken and/or recorded by Matthew.

The basic structure of Matthew is rather simple: it alternates blocks of narrative (story) material with large sections of teaching material. There are five such teaching sections (usually called "discourses"): the Sermon on the Mount (chaps. 5-7); Jesus' missionary instructions to the Twelve (chap. 10); "parables of the kingdom" (chap. 13); and the "eschatological discourse," in which Jesus speaks of the destruction of Jerusalem and the eventual coming of the Son of Man (chaps. 24-25). Matthew 18 is the fourth of these five discourses, and its theme is "Relationships within the Kingdom Community." The first verses of chapters 18 and 19 show that this is a connected series of instructions ("At that time" — 18:1; "Now when Jesus had finished these sayings" — 19:1), and the contents suggest that there is but one overall theme. Chapter 18 discusses how followers of Jesus, beginning with the apostles but not limited to them, are to interact with and treat one another. The communal aspects of this section of teaching are highlighted by the fact that this is one of only two places in Matthew where the word "church" (*ekklesia*) occurs (18:17; the other is 16:18), and that Matthew is the only one of the four Gospels to contain this word at all. Jesus apparently knew that one of the greatest challenges confronting the new communities of believers would be in the personal realm: how do we get along with one another and help one another attain the spiritual goals laid out for us by our Lord? "Within such a community there is opportunity both to harm and to care for others, and the health and effectiveness of the group will depend on the attitudes to one another which are fostered."[2]

Our text occurs about the middle of the chapter, so let's back up and see how it all begins. Interestingly, it begins with a conflict situation among the disciples: "At that time the disciples came to Jesus, saying, 'Who is the greatest in the kingdom of heaven?'" A careful reading of the Synoptic Gospels reveals that the disciples are asking this question about themselves (that is, "Which of *us* is the greatest?"), and that this was far from the only time that they discussed it. Mark 9:33-37 relates an incident when Jesus asked them, "What were you discussing on the way?" But they were too embarrassed to tell him, "for on the way they had discussed with one another who was the greatest." And this just after he had predicted for the second time his own suffering, death, and resurrection (Mk. 9:30-32)! Then, there was the time when the mother of James and John came to Jesus and asked him to give her sons the most prominent positions in his coming kingdom. After Jesus informed both mother and sons that such a request was not his to grant, Matthew tells us that when the other ten disciples heard it, "they were indignant" (Matt. 20:24). Apparently they coveted these choice places for themselves. Luke relates that even in the midst of the Last Supper, as Jesus spoke of his impending betrayal and death, that "a dispute also arose among them, which of them was to be regarded as the greatest" (Lk. 22:24).[3] Clearly, the desire for prominence and power in the kingdom is nothing new. Nor, unfortunately, has it gotten much better after nineteen hundred years.[4]

Jesus responds by presenting a child as the model for them to emulate. They must "turn and become like children" in order even to be *in* his kingdom, and "he who humbles himself like this child, he is the greatest in the kingdom of heaven" (18:2-4). Obviously, the standards of greatness in Jesus' kingdom were going to be far different than in the world at large. The point of the child model is not, as often claimed, innocence. Rather, as stated in verse 4, humility is the supreme kingdom virtue, but humility in a particular sense. Children in Jewish society were objects of great affection, but they had absolutely no status, no "rights" beyond what the adults in their lives extended to them.[5] So, Jesus is teaching the disciples that they must become devoid of the desire for status and power; such is true greatness in the kingdom of him who emptied himself of all privilege in order to be our Savior (see Phil. 2:5-11).

The next section of the discourse (vs. 5-11), continuing the theme of child-likeness, concerns the willingness of disciples to accept all other disciples, regardless of their apparent insignificance. Jesus expresses concern that disciples "receive" *all* of his "little ones" (believers) and that they not cause them to sin, either through direct temptation or by failing to accept them and thus pushing them outside the community. "Receive" in this context means to "accept as infinitely valuable."[6] The disciples are warned not to "despise" (look down upon, count as of no value) one of these little ones, because even the most insignificant has his/her representation in heaven and is deeply cared for by "my Father who is in heaven" (vs. 10-11). This is a stinging rebuke to what happens so often in churches, when some members are deemed to be less important than others. As Douglas Hare has written, "How easy it is for the active members of a church to ignore those who play no leadership role and contribute only modestly to the budget!"[7]

This concern for all of Christ's followers is then illustrated by the Parable of the Lost Sheep (vs. 12-14). These verses are extremely important, because they immediately precede Jesus' words about discipline and so form their immediate context. The point of the parable is not, as often supposed, to demonstrate that Jesus or God is the Good Shepherd who cares for every one of his sheep. That _is_ the point of the parable as told in Luke 15, but not here. The point has already been stated forcibly in verse 10: "See that _you_ do not despise one of these little ones." The "good shepherd" motif represents the concern that Jesus expects every believer to have for every other believer. It is in this sense that we are to be "keepers" of one another. The shepherd's unwillingness to "write off" even one of his sheep shows that every one in the kingdom is important to God (v. 14) and so must be to us. In the kingdom of God, we have no right to discount or disregard the worth of any one. No one is "dispensable." We are no more permitted to disregard our brother than to cause him to sin (vs. 7-9)! "So it is not the will of my Father who is in heaven that one of these little ones should perish."

Our neglect in this regard is painfully obvious: How often does it happen in the church that people just disappear without notice? We speak of "fringe members" and people who "fall through the cracks," as though such things were the expected norm and need not concern us unduly.[8] Jesus says it should _never_ happen. We should be able to account for every sheep, because every one belongs to God and is of inestimable value. Perhaps the first step to godly discipline in the church ought to be repentance over our indifference toward so many of God's sheep. And this is not just the responsibility of elders, as we shall see later, but of every disciple.

It is this strong teaching about congregational concern for the individual which leads to Jesus' words about disciplining the erring. It is essential that we keep this context firmly in mind, so that we will cease to think of verses 15-17 as simply outlining a disciplinary "procedure." Rather, we must recognize them as describing a means of _regaining those who become lost_, for preserving them intact within the Christian family. The steps outlined in verses 15-17 are the Christ-ordained way of refusing to allow people to disappear from the church as if they were never among us.

The remainder of chapter 18 continues the theme of infinite concern, with Peter's question about how often he must forgive his brother (vs. 21-22), and Jesus' reply — as often as necessary. This teaching is then reinforced with the Parable of the Unmerciful Servant (vs. 23-35), one of Jesus' most powerful stories. Its lesson is clear: "Don't you *dare* drive any one out of the kingdom by refusing to forgive!"

So the message of the entire chapter is a rebuke to the spirit of self-seeking and -serving and emphasizes that in Jesus' kingdom everyone, no matter how insignificant from a worldly perspective, is important. And so it's required of every member of the kingdom to be concerned for the spiritual welfare of every other member, even to the point of personal confrontation about sin. *No one* is expendable!

1. Keep in mind that the "later" statements, such as those of Paul, were probably written down before Jesus' words were written. There can be little question, however, that Jesus' words were already widely known in their oral form and influenced what was eventually written in the New Testament letters.

2. R. T. France, *The Gospel According to Matthew* (Grand Rapids: Eerdmans, 1985) 269.

3. It was probably this disputing at the table which prompted Jesus to arise and wash the disciples' feet, as recorded in John 13.

4. C. E. B. Cranfield, *The Gospel According to Saint Mark* (Cambridge: University Press, 1966) says that "the question of precedence was specially important in Palestine and was incessantly arising, whether in the synagogue service or judicial proceedings or at meals" (34).

5. "In modern Western societies children are often seen as very important, but in first-century Judaism they were not. . . . In the affairs of men children were unimportant. They could not fight, they could not lead, they had not had time to acquire worldly wisdom, they could not pile up riches, they counted for very little. To speak of them as humble is surely a reference to their small size rather than any intellectual or spiritual virtue. Their smallness made them very humble members of society" (Leon Morris, *The Gospel According to Matthew* [Grand Rapids: Eerdmans, 1992] 60).

6. Douglas R. A. Hare, *Matthew* (Louisville: John Knox, 1993) 211.

7.   Hare, 212.

8.   "The temptation for the spiritually serious is to look down on half-hearted or 'nominal' Christians, on people to whom Jesus Christ seems to mean too little. Fourth-soil Christians find it hard to like the other three soils" (F. D. Bruner, *Matthew*, Vol. 2 [Dallas: Word, 1990] 641).

FOR THOUGHT AND DISCUSSION

1. What aspects of American culture encourage us to feel that we are not our brother's keeper?

2. Explain why Matthew 18:15-17 is such an important text in the discussion of church discipline.

3. How does the disciples' question about "who was the greatest" fit into the context of Matthew 18?

4. How many people are on the "membership roll" of the church where you worship whose presence cannot be accounted for? Why does this happen? What can be done to correct this situation?

5. Are there members of your congregation who could easily "slip through the cracks" through the neglect of others? Why? What should be done to prevent this from happening?

"My brothers, if any one among you wanders from the truth and some one brings him back, let him know that whoever brings back a sinner from the error of his way will save his soul from death and will cover a multitude of sins."

— James 5:19-20

"IF YOUR BROTHER SINS. . . ."

(MATTHEW 18:15-17)

We now turn our attention to Jesus' specific instructions about reclaiming the erring brother.[1] Because this text is so important to our understanding of discipline, and because the context is so important for understanding this text, please be sure that you have read the preceding chapter before beginning this one.

Jesus begins, "If your brother sins. . ." (v. 15). He leaves us in no doubt that people in God's kingdom must take sin seriously. It can scarcely be denied that today's church seldom takes sin as seriously as Jesus' words say that we should. Perhaps it is our American "live and let live" mentality, our rugged independence, our sense of minding one's own business that causes us to fail in this matter so consistently. But we must also confess a spiritual insensitivity to sin. We don't want to see sin in ourselves, and it is much easier simply to "let it slide" in the lives of others. But to do so is to fail to take seriously the destructive nature of sin. Jesus' words will not allow us this luxury.

Note that Jesus speaks of our "brother's" sin. Some commentators see a shift at this point from the discussion about Jesus' "little ones" earlier in the chapter to matters concerning one's "brother."[2] But this misses the point of Matthew 18 entirely, because it destroys the unity of thought in the discourse. Our "brother" *is* one of Jesus' "little ones" and thus not to be despised, sinned against, ignored, or left to perish in his sin. Our relationship as fellow-citizens of Christ's kingdom requires action in the event of a brother's sin.

An important question arises at this point: Did Jesus say, "If your brother *sins*. . .", or "If your brother sins *against you*. . ."? The words "against you" are present in most of the ancient Greek manuscripts, but they are missing in some important ones. This is reflected in the various English translations. The King James, Revised Standard, New Revised Standard, New International, and Today's English versions, plus J. B. Phillips' translation include the phrase (though some of these have notes indicating the variation). The New American Standard Bible, Jerusalem Bible, New English Bible, and Revised English Bible omit it. The commentaries are fairly evenly divided on the question, with perhaps a slight majority favoring the omission of "against you."[3] If the words were not originally in Matthew's text, they were probably added by a later scribe who was familiar with the parallel in Luke 17:4: ". . . and if he sins against you seven times in the day, and turns to you seven times, and says, 'I repent,' you must forgive him."[4] Likewise, Peter's question in verse 21 might suggest that a personal offense is under consideration in verse 15, and this could have influenced an early copyist to add "against you." On the whole it seems best to omit "against you," but this must be said with caution.

But does it make any difference? Possibly a great deal. Some conclude that Jesus' words — and the obligation to confront the sinner personally — apply only if the offense is personal in nature. So, if the sin is not "against me," then I am excused from the requirement to go to the sinning brother and am permitted, in the view of some, to discuss his sin with others. This question frequently arises in situations where someone has concluded that another brother is a "false teacher." Since false teaching is not a "personal" offense, the accuser is then at liberty to openly criticize the accused, even in print. Such an attitude clearly violates the spirit of this text and of its context, and is often only an excuse for not confronting someone with whom we disagree. As we will see later, Paul takes a different stance toward "outside agitators" than toward those who are part of the Christian community, but never does he suggest that any "brother" is unworthy of our efforts to reclaim him, or that the label "false teacher" is a license to verbally kill! (See Tit. 3:10-11 for a pertinent example. Even the pervertedly divisive are to be warned.)[5] But even if the words "against you" are judged to be original, this does not excuse any of us from failing to approach a brother or sister who is involved in sin — any sin, even false teaching. Bound together in the Christian fellowship as we are, there is a sense in which *all* sin is "against me." But the primary thrust of Jesus' words is not toward determining who is offended, but reclaiming the offender. We shouldn't quibble about words when people's reputations — or even their souls — are at stake.[6]

A somewhat troubling aspect of this passage is that Jesus does not specify precisely what sins or what kinds of sins require our attention. Surely we are not to think that we are to approach a brother about any and every mistake we might see in his life. So the question remains, "At what point should one believer intervene in the life of another?" Sometimes the answer given is that only sins of a *public* nature require intervention. But Jesus didn't say, "If your brother sins publicly. . . , " and the concern for privacy expressed in verse 15 would seem to rule this out as being either the sole or primary criterion. Likewise, the claim that the sin must be both serious and intentional finds no support in the text.[7] And since Galatians 6:1 specifies "any sin" in which a brother or sister might be ensnared, perhaps we should be cautious in trying to delineate too sharply which sins require action and which do not.

Still, I'd like to suggest some criteria for deciding to "go to a brother." One is the seriousness of a particular sin. While it's certainly true that "a sin is a sin," it is equally true that not all sins are equal in their impact on the sinner, the church, and the watching community (see I Cor. 5 for an example). Being unfaithful to one's wife or husband is hardly in the same category as breaking the speed limit.[8] Another factor to be considered is whether someone has simply committed a "mistake," or is practicing a sin habitually, regardless of its "seriousness." While a failure to attend worship is a matter of concern, the habitual "forsaking of the assembly" would certainly demand attention. Likewise, if a particular behavior is grossly inconsistent with the nature of the Christian life, it should be addressed, as Paul does in Ephesians 5 and Colossians 3, in dealing with various forms of immorality. These are certainly not hard-and-fast rules, and are in no way intended to belittle the seriousness of any sin, but perhaps they will provide some guidelines for deciding whether to act. Also, in the following chapters, we will encounter texts which speak of specific sins requiring discipline, and these will be invaluable guides in making such determinations.

It goes without saying that deciding whether to confront someone about sin will inevitably be a matter of judgment, and always should be approached in a prayerful manner.

"Go and tell him his fault"

In a situation where sin becomes known to us, we are to act in a very specific manner: "tell him his fault, between you and him alone." This is an extremely important first step, but one which is often ignored. Our tendency is either to do nothing at all about our brother's sin, or else to tell others about it. But seldom do we do exactly as Jesus says by going to the offender privately. Jesus' teaching suggests that we should deal with the problem at the lowest possible level, by involving no more people than necessary. Why is this aura of privacy so important? For one thing, we may find that our information about our brother's behavior was incorrect or wrongly interpreted. And if he is guilty of some particular sin, we should try to avoid embarrassing him unnecessarily.

The verb *elenchein* ("tell him his fault") means to bring to light, expose something, or to point out something to someone, to reprove and correct. (See, for example, its use in Lk. 3:19, I Cor. 14:24, II Tim. 4:2, Tit. 1:9.) It need not include strong rebuke or severe judgment, but simply an exposure of guilt, done in such a way as to induce repentance.[9] This is a delicate task, as any one who has ever tried it can attest, and it is best accomplished exactly as Jesus says — *alone.*

"If he listens. . ."

Jesus immediately reminds us of the goal of going to our brother: to "gain" him. In the New Testament this term usually refers to material gain. But here it aptly expresses the goal of all remedial church discipline: to get back into the fold people who may have wandered out. And it reminds us of the spirit in which such an effort must be undertaken, one of hopeful expectation of winning our brother back — not of "telling him off" and/or "getting rid" of him. Going to our brother privately is not simply the "first step toward disfellowshipping" him. It is, hopefully, the only step needed to "gain" him. Each of the actions here taught by Jesus is complete within itself and may be sufficient for regaining our brother. We should, therefore, pursue each one as if it alone will be sufficient, not in anticipation of a negative outcome requiring further action.

"But if he does not listen. . ."

Not surprisingly, people usually don't like to hear about their sins, even when they're clearly in the wrong. Even the kindest, most humble effort at reproving may meet with rejection rather than appreciation. Human nature would tell us to give up at this point. But Jesus tells us to press on. Our brother is too important for us simply to walk away after a first refusal.

The instruction to take one or two others with us, "that every word may be confirmed by the evidence of two or three witnesses,"[10] is not as much of a "judicial" act as it may sound. Note the continued concern for privacy — just one or two, not as many as we can round up. And their function is not to serve as "witnesses for the prosecution, " but for the protection of both the offending brother and the one trying to reclaim him. Quite often in such confrontations, meanings can be twisted, intentions misinterpreted, and previous statements misquoted. The "witnesses, " who were not privy to the initial meeting between the two parties, can add balance and offer guidance and judgment for the ongoing discussion. Also, in the event that they determine that the accused person is, indeed, in the wrong, they can add their own appeal for repentance. As the beginning of verse 17 suggests, the goal is still reclamation, not dismissal. The witnesses are "to deprive the sinner of the later excuse that his accuser is biased or pursuing a selfish goal, is reproving him unjustly or in anger. . . . In a real sense they are to be adduced *for* the sinner, rather than *against* him."[11]

"Tell it to the church"

If repeated efforts at restoration fail, the circle of those involved must be widened. Jesus says, "tell it to the church." Hopefully it will not go this far, but if it does, we must not shrink from doing as Jesus instructs, in hope that the offender will listen to the combined voices of the entire church. "Telling it to the church" is not simply an announcement of a decision made by the elders or someone else. Rather, it is a call to the entire congregation to become involved in the very serious task of restoring a brother before it is too late. Our Lord could not have more clearly emphasized the responsibility of every Christian to be involved in the disciplinary process. The whole church is to be active in discipline for the added effect of a united appeal ("if he refuses to listen to the church"). Also, in the unfortunate event that withdrawal of fellowship becomes necessary, everyone can "own" the decision. It is extremely important that this phase of the restoration process not be overlooked, otherwise considerable confusion and unrest may result among those who are uninformed about why the decision was made. Withdrawing the church's fellowship is *never* the prerogative of a few, but the responsibility of the entire body. Except in some extremely delicate cases, it is a decision that should be made *by* the church and not *for* it.[12]

"As a Gentile and a tax collector"

When all other attempts at restoration have failed, it is time for "radical surgery." The sinning Christian who refuses even the appeals of the united congregation must be deprived of the church's fellowship.[13] "Gentiles" and "tax collectors" were categories of "unclean" people who were to be avoided by Jews. Such avoidance not only expressed disapproval but also prevented contamination. Both aspects seem to be in view in verse 17b. But even such drastic action has a positive intent — the hope that the sinning Christian will be grieved by the ostracism of his brothers and sisters and long to be included once again in the fellowship of the church. But if he does not, at least the church is preserved from his negative influence.[14]

"Whatever you bind on earth. . ."

While we often hear much about verses 15-17 in discussions of church discipline, we usually hear very little, if anything, about verses 18-20. Yet they are an inherent part of the subject and have some important points to make, as important as the "procedural" discussion in the previous verses.

For one thing, verse 18 informs us that when the congregation unites in disciplinary action, it does so on behalf of God himself, because we are thereby seeking to put into practice the teachings of his word. In addition, the church is assured that its actions are ratified by Heaven itself. This is not to suggest that the church can "make up the rules as we go along," but rather, "as the church is responsive to the guidance of God it will come to the decisions that have already been made in heaven."[15] The "two agreeing" of verse 19 is not, as we usually hear, about agreeing in prayer, but about agreeing on the proper course of discipline. Likewise, the "two or three" gathered in Christ's name is not a promise about our corporate worship (although the statement would certainly be true in that context), but a promise about our disciplinary decisions.[16] The solemn act of congregational discipline is not only ratified by Jesus, but he participates with us in it, even as we do it. Perhaps it might help us in carrying out the difficult task of congregational discipline to remember that, "Church discipline is not an action of merely human administration: it may count on the assistance and ratification of the risen Christ."[17] It is by his command that we discipline, and it is with his help that we carry out what he has commanded.

But what has all of this to do with the themes of holiness, fellowship, and truth-telling which we identified at the outset as underlying all that the New Testament teaches about discipline? By now, that should be obvious. Holiness and truthfulness demand that we not be a people who ignore sin in our own lives or in our midst as a community of believers. They demand that when sin does occur, as it inevitably will, we must be willing to face up to it and attempt to rectify it, regardless of the difficulty. They even demand that, on occasion, we will separate ourselves from fellow-believers whose lives are out of harmony with our Lord's teachings and who cannot be made to see that they are so. Matthew 18:15-17, and indeed the entire chapter, reminds us that we can only "share his holiness" if we are willing to confront sin truthfully and remove it from our midst. But fellowship demands that we not do so too quickly or unlovingly, that we show the same care and concern for one weak, unattractive sheep that we would show for any other. It demands that we act as inconspicuously and discreetly as possible in order to preserve our brother's reputation and integrity. But it also demands that we act in concert as a body of believers to reclaim stubborn wanderers from the fold. And it reminds us that as we do this in fellowship with one another, we are also doing so in fellowship with our Lord himself.

1. No apology is necessary for retaining Jesus' use of the masculine reference, while recognizing that his words apply equally to both sexes. As noted previously, the NRSV seriously blurs the fellowship aspect of Jesus' words by translating *adelphos* (brother) as "another member of the church" and "that one" in v. 15, and by using "the member," "the offender," and "such a one" in place of the masculine pronoun in vs. 15-17. This is unnecessary and creates a clumsy translation of a rather straightforward paragraph.

2. See, for example, W. D. Davies and Dale C. Allison, Jr., *A Critical and Exegetical Commentary on the Gospel According to Saint Matthew*, Vol. II (Edinburgh: T & T Clark, 1991) 750-51; and Daniel J. Harrington, *The Gospel of Matthew* (Collegeville, Minn.: The Liturgical Press, 1991) 265.

3. B. M. Metzger, *A Textual Commentary on the Greek New Testament* (United Bible Societies, 1971) 45, categorizes the variation as having a "considerable degree of doubt" about which reading is correct.

4. Lk. 17:1-4 is a close parallel to Matt.18:15-17 and should be studied in combination with it. The passage in Lk. seems to be something of a capsule summary of the Matthean text, and emphasizes likewise the concern for not causing others to sin in the context of an overall view of Christian relationships.

5. It should be observed that although Paul frequently speaks out boldly against false teachings and teachers, only rarely does he mention people by name. This may be due to the fact that his readers already know about whom he is speaking. But it may also be a deliberate attempt to keep attention focused on the error rather than creating a clash over personalities, and to avoid sinning against brothers whom he had not had the opportunity to confront personally. I Tim. 1:18-20 and II Tim. 4:14-15 are exceptions to Paul's general practice, and in both instances Paul had had personal confrontations with the people named. In other cases he can speak quite harshly about false teachers and opponents, but does not name them, even though he apparently knows who they are (see, e.g., Phil. 3:2ff, Rom. 3:8, II Cor. 10:10-12, 11:12-15).

6. See, for example, Gal. 6:1, which specifies that "any sin" in which a brother

is overtaken demands our efforts at restoration. G.W. H. Lampe, "Church Discipline and the Interpretation of the Epistles to the Corinthians," *Christian History and Interpretation: Studies Presented to John Knox*, ed. by W. R. Farmer *et al* (Cambridge: University Press, 1967), argues that it is clear that Matt. 18:15-17 is not dealing only with personal offenses, because these are dealt with in 18:21ff "by the very different method of unlimited forgiveness" (345).

7.   This is the view of Davies and Allison, 782. Even wider of the mark is the claim of Daniel J. Harrington that "The biblical procedure presupposes a criminal offence, not a problem within a community" (269).

8.   "Matthew's view of sin is strong in that it preserves us from that moral twilight in which all cats are gray, in which no sins are more serious than others, and so over which a mist of indifference can hang ('after all, we all sin')" (Bruner, 646).

9.   William G. Thompson, *Matthew's Advice to a Divided Community* (Rome: Biblical Institute Press, 1970) 178. Such texts as Prov. 3:12, Job 5:17, Heb. 12:5, etc. "depict God as One who educates by correction" (F. Buchsel, "*elencho, etc.*," *Theological Dictionary of the New Testament*, One Volume edition, ed. by G. W. Bromiley [Grand Rapids: Eerdmans, 1985] 222).

10.   Evidently derived from Deut. 19:15.

11.   Victor C. Pfitzner, "Purified Community — Purified Sinner," *Australian Biblical Review* No. 30 [1982] 39.

12.   But, as we will see in our study of some of Paul's texts on discipline, all of these "steps" are not required as a pattern for all cases (e.g., I Cor. 5, Tit. 3:10-11).

13.   Some maintain that "let him be to you" refers only to the original accuser and not to the church as a whole, because the Greek pronoun "you" (*soi*) is singular and not plural. However, the earlier involvement of the church in the process and the switch to the second person plural in v. 18 show that this is to be a communal, and not merely a personal, act. R. H. Gundry, *Matthew: A Commentary on His Literary and Theological Art* (Grand Rapids: Eerdmans, 1982) 368.

14.   On the entire subject of the expected results of such disciplinary action, see the discussion of I Cor. 5 in Chapter 9.

15.   Leon Morris, *The Gospel According to Matthew* (Grand Rapids: Eerdmans,

1992) 469. R. T. France adds that the church's refusal to overlook sin without rebuke carries with it the prior endorsement of heaven (*The Gospel According to Matthew* [Grand Rapids: Eerdmans, 1985] 275).

16. According to J. D. M. Derrett, the phrase "where two or three are gathered together" has nothing to do with prayer. Rather, "It means that unofficial dispute settlers, peacemakers, perform a divine function" ("'Where two or three are convened in my name. . .': a sad misunderstanding,*"* *Expository Times* No. 91 [1979] 86).

17. David Hill, *The Gospel of Matthew* (London: Oliphants, 1972) 276.

FOR THOUGHT AND DISCUSSION

1.   How does Matthew 18:15-17 show that sin should be taken seriously?

2.   What criteria could you add for determining under what circumstances we should approach a sinning brother or sister?

3.   In what ways does Jesus remind us in Matthew 18:15-17 that the goal of discipline is to restore the sinner rather than to remove him/her?

4.   Why is it important to keep discipline as private as possible?

5.   Have you ever personally gone to a brother or sister in the way Jesus describes? What was the result of your efforts? What would you do differently if faced with the same situation again?

"So then be neither consenting to evil, so as to approve it; nor negligent so as not to reprove it; nor proud so as to reprove it in a tone of insult."

— Augustine of Hippo

GENTLE RESTORATION

(GALATIANS 6:1)

For years Irene had been one of the stalwarts of the church. An accomplished teacher and zealous personal evangelist, she had been instrumental in leading numerous people to Christ and was admired by all the congregation. In every respect, her life was a model of Christian faithfulness and service. Then one day, word began to circulate around town that Irene had been accused of stealing money from her employer. She didn't deny the charges, and, because she was a long-time employee, they were eventually dropped. Irene just moved on to another job and stopped attending church. Everyone in· the congregation was stunned—so stunned, in fact, that no one said or did anything about the situation. There were murmurings and whispered conversations, but no one approached Irene to discuss her sin. They were all too shocked. How could this happen to someone like Irene?

When people whose faith we admire disappoint us in such drastic ways, it creates a spiritual shock that is hard to absorb. We're prone to think that surely this person was a hypocrite all along, that his or her profession of faith was false from the start, that "true Christians" simply can't commit such awful acts, and that anyone who would do such a thing is no longer worthy of our concern. We forget about the power of what Paul calls "the flesh," that tendency resident within us all that would cause us to act selfishly and pull us away from God. According to Romans 8 and Galatians 5, the flesh is an ever-present danger whose power we dare not under-estimate. As the example of David, a "man after God's own heart," well testifies, even the best of God's servants is capable of shameful behavior. Our only hope is to trust in Christ and not in ourselves, and to discipline ourselves to "walk by the Spirit" so that we will not "gratify the desires of the flesh."

But what happens when one among us doesn't follow the Spirit's way, when we allow the flesh to have its way? What about someone like Irene? Can she be reclaimed, or must we simply write her off as a tragic loss? Do we have any responsibility to her, or has her behavior made her unworthy of our efforts?

Flesh vs. Spirit

It is clear from the beginning of Galatians that Paul is writing to combat what he considers a drastic deviation from the gospel he had preached to the Galatian churches. In 1:6 he expresses astonishment that they have, within a relatively short period of time, abandoned his teaching and have embraced "a different gospel." He goes on to explain that this is not really another gospel but only a perversion of the one gospel (1:7), and pronounces an "anathema" (a sentence of condemnation) upon anyone guilty of preaching a gospel contrary to his original message (1:8-9). As you read through the letter, the nature of the problem becomes clearer. It involves a conflict over justification, whether we are made right with God by works of the law or through faith in Christ (2:15-16). The seriousness of this issue becomes evident in 3:10, as Paul quotes Deuteronomy 27:26 to support his contention that "all who rely on works of the law are under a curse." Further, it becomes clear in 5:2 and 6:12 that the crux of the issue was not the law of Moses in its entirety, but circumcision.

So the situation is this: some unidentified persons, obviously Jewish Christians, were attempting to force the observance of the law on the Galatian Christians, who were mostly Gentiles. Obviously this demand was not presented in place of the gospel, but in addition to it (5:2). Of particular concern to these "Judaizers," as they are usually called, was that the Galatians must submit to circumcision. Paul charges in 6:13 that this is the real issue and not the law as such. Apparently these Jewish Christians were being persecuted for associating with uncircumcised Gentiles in the church (6:12). If the Gentiles would only accept circumcision, the tension between these Jewish believers and their non-Christian Jewish neighbors would be resolved. But Paul sees this as a serious breach of the basic principle of the gospel — that is, that justification can come only through faith in Christ — and he condemns it in no uncertain terms. He takes great pains to show that justification cannot possibly come through the law (2:21-4:31) and issues a stirring call to freedom: "For freedom Christ has set us free; stand fast therefore, and do not submit again to a yoke of slavery" (5:1). If the Galatians are to escape the slavery of law-keeping, they must insist on their freedom in Christ.

But freedom always runs the risk of turning into libertinism, the attitude which says, "Because of Christ and God's grace, I can do anything I want." We know from Romans 3:8 and 6:1-2 that there were people in Paul's own day who were saying just that (or, accusing Paul of teaching it; see also I Cor. 10:23ff). So, along with his call to freedom, Paul also issues a call to moral and ethical responsibility: "For you were called to freedom, brethren; only do not use your freedom as an opportunity for the flesh, but through love be servants of one another" (5:13). And from this point on through 6:10, he gives a series of instructions designed to combat the libertinistic attitude. He shows particular concern for the way Christians treat one another. In fact, his instructions about "walking by the Spirit" rather than "by the flesh" are framed by statements of a relational nature: "For the whole law is fulfilled in one word, 'You shall love your neighbor as yourself.' But if you bite and devour one another take heed that you are not consumed by one another" (5:14-15). "Let us have no conceit, no provoking of one another, no envy of one another" (5:26). It may be that Paul knew of particular problems of this kind among the Galatians, or he may simply be aware that libertinism inevitably results in the abuse of one's privileges at the expense of others.

It is in this context of warning the Galatians not to use their liberty as license that Paul admonishes them to exercise discipline. He has already urged upon them the necessity of "walking by the Spirit" (5:16ff), which involves a spirit of humility and a concern for others' welfare. This concern must continue, Paul says, even when (perhaps *especially* when) a fellow Christian has fallen into sinful behavior.

> Brothers, even if a person is overtaken in some trespass, you who are spiritual restore such a one with a gentle spirit, looking out for yourself, lest you also be tempted (Gal. 6:1; author's translation).

We should notice right away the similarities between Paul's teaching and that of Jesus in Matthew 18:15-17 (see Chapters 5 and 6). In both texts the general concern is for Christian relationships. Both teach the necessity of a humble spirit toward one another. And both emphasize that even sin in someone's life does not make him/her unworthy of our love and attention, but rather calls for the concern of each individual and of the group as a whole in order to restore them to wholeness in their relationship with both God and the rest of the church.

Overtaken in Sin

As in the case of Jesus' instructions, Paul speaks of "sin" in a very general fashion, rather than of any specific situation. Any time one of the "brothers" fails to "walk by the Spirit, " then there is a problem which requires attention from the larger group. There are two categories of church members in view here. One is "you who are spiritual," and the other is anyone who is "overtaken in sin." We should not misinterpret "the spiritual" to mean some "super-spiritual" faction within the Galatian churches, such as evidently existed at Corinth. The context requires us to understand "the spiritual" as simply those who *are* walking by the Spirit as Paul directed in 5:16-26. So the "spiritual" are the church as a whole who are consistently practicing Christian principles. The other category of church member is the one who will on occasion deviate seriously from Christian practices, in other words, who is not "walking by the Spirit" — someone like Irene. This person Paul describes as having been "overtaken in some trespass." The word translated "overtaken" (*prolambano*) may suggest either that the person has been inadvertently involved in wrong-doing, or that he/she has been "surprised" or "detected" in sin by another Christian. In neither case is the trespass excusable, although the former sense would indicate that the individual did not deliberately set out to do what he/she ended up doing. Regardless of the precise intention of Paul's verb, however, his overall meaning is clear: the one who falls into sin cannot simply be ignored by the rest. Such people are certainly not beyond hope, regardless of the shocking nature of their sin. And their sin must be recognized and dealt with appropriately.

Restore Such a One

What action should be taken by "the spiritual?" We might expect to find here a repetition of Jesus' words from Matthew 18, that is, the "steps" toward regaining a sinner. In fact, as we will see later, Paul never quotes the words of Jesus from Matthew 18 precisely, as if he regarded them as some sort of legal formula which must be followed to the letter in every case.

In this instance the required action is summed up in the single verb, "restore," which is Paul's term for bringing back the erring Christian to the Spirit's way. The verb *kartartizo* is used in Matthew 4:21 and Mark 1:19 for the mending of fish nets, in I Corinthians 1:10 as a term for Christian unity, and II Corinthians 13:11 in an appeal to "mend your ways." It has the connotation of restoring someone or something to proper order. And isn't that the goal of discipline, as we have seen so far — to restore someone to a life of walking by the Spirit rather than by the flesh? To restore him to fellowship with God and with his people? To restore fractured relationships within the church when they have been disrupted by sin? While Paul says nothing about the *process* of "restoration," he focuses on the ultimate *goal* of that process — in Jesus' words, "regaining your brother." Once again, we are reminded of the real purpose of discipline, not to punish or eliminate or control, but to restore. And we can readily see how Jesus' teachings fit under the umbrella of Paul's verb "restore." Going to a sinning Christian privately, involving others in our efforts to persuade, telling it to the church — even avoidance — all are aimed at the restoration of broken lives and broken relationships.

With a Gentle Spirit

Now, if this is to he done effectively, we must go about it in a specific manner: "in a spirit of gentleness," or, "with a gentle spirit." Those who are walking by the Spirit must not assume an attitude of spiritual superiority to those overtaken in sin. It is not a case of "the righteous" pointing the accusing finger at "the sinful" (another reason to prefer the translation "overtaken" rather than "caught"). The spiritual are to go with a deep sense of gentle humility to those who were once spiritual like themselves, yet who have fallen into "fleshly" ways. In fact, Paul goes on to caution the spiritual to "Look to yourself, lest you too be tempted." We are never in a proper frame of mind to deal with other people's sins until we are deeply conscious of our own weaknesses and failings. Only then can we have the proper spirit ot humility and gentleness, as "one beggar to another." In this way, and in this spirit, we can truly "bear one another's burdens" (v. 2).

What does all of this say about our failures to restore one another when necessary? Surely we must admit that not much of this goes on in today's church! What are the implications of our failure? Obviously, it suggests that we are not taking sin as seriously as Jesus and Paul did. We are prone not to act unless forced to do so; as long as the surface of the waters appears untroubled, we are content to ignore the dangerous currents beneath. Another implication is that we fail to acknowledge the distinction between those who walk by the Spirit and those who do not. Paul says that "the works of the flesh are *plain*" (5:19), but we sometimes act as if no one can possibly discern who is sinning and who isn't. Still another implication is the implicit denial of our fellowship — that we are, in fact, spiritually bound together and obligated to one another. "Brother" and "sister" are not just titles — they suggest relationships, and relationship implies responsibility, *our* responsibility to act when a fellow-Christian is in trouble.

There's really no question what the church *should* have done when Irene left the Spirit's way: her brothers and sisters should have sought to restore her with a gentle spirit. Such sin in the life of a Christian is a terrible thing, but it is not necessarily fatal. People *do* actually repent, and when they do, they are forgiven. And it may well be that our loving confrontation, gently and humbly stated, will be all that it takes to bring someone like Irene back to her Lord and to his people.

APPENDIX A

GALATIANS 1:8-9: "AN INSTANCE OF EARLY CHURCH DISCIPLINE"?

It is amazing that many students of Galatians fail to recognize that 6:1 is a text about congregational discipline. This is largely due to a presupposition about the nature of early Christian discipline, found commonly in New Testament scholarship, that leads to a badly distorted misunderstanding of Scripture. Simply put, this presupposition is that the early church employed curses against offenders in their midst which resulted in (or were expected to result in) their deaths. Support for this view is claimed on the basis of passages such as Acts 5:1-11 (the punitive deaths of Ananias and Sapphira) and I Corinthians 11:29-30 (failure to "discern the body" at the Lord's Supper resulting in illness and death). Further discussion of this point of view will accompany our study of I Corinthians 5, since "deliver... to Satan" in that chapter is also interpreted as a curse/death situation.

Following this line of thought, some scholars interpret Galatians 1:8-9 as a "typical" text on early church discipline. Paul pronounces the "anathema" on those who preach another gospel, supposedly expecting them to die as a result. In his highly influential commentary on Galatians, Hans Dieter Betz describes Galatians 1:8-9 as "an instance of early church discipline" and "the first instance of Christian excommunication,"[1] based on the occurrence of "anathema" in some ancient Greek magical texts. He has been followed in this interpretation by many others.[2]

First, it should be noted that Paul's use of "anathema" is based not on Greek magical texts, but on the Septuagint (the Old Testament in Greek), where it appears frequently. In the Old Testament "anathema" is used to designate that which is "devoted to the Lord for destruction" (see, for example, Josh. 6:17, Num. 21:3, Ezra 10:8). The point of Paul's use of the term is to proclaim the law of God which is operative under certain conditions: that is, if anyone preaches a different gospel, he automatically falls under God's curse — not the church's or Paul's. He does not intend by his curse to bring about the sentence of condemnation; he merely announces the way things are.

Second, the following points should be observed concerning the claim that Galatians 1:8-9 is a text on church discipline:

(1) There is no evidence that "anathema" was ever used in a disciplinary sense in the first century. It was used in this way in later centuries, primarily by Roman Catholics, but not until long after Paul's time. (See, for example, Romans 9:3 and I Corinthians 12:3, where this sense is obviously excluded.)

(2) Paul's statement in Galatians 1:8-9 does not call for any corporate act on the part of the church.

(3) The pagan texts which supposedly serve as models for a disciplinary understanding of Galatians 1:8-9 are not disciplinary in nature. "They were apparently simply pronounced by angry people who wished evil and misery upon some luckless enemy."[3]

(4) There is no supporting evidence that Paul or any of the churches under his influence used curses in the exercise of church discipline.[4]

The curse/death understanding of church discipline is clearly to be rejected as a serious distortion of what early Christian discipline was all about. Instead, we must look to texts such as Galatians 6:1, which carry forward the teaching of Jesus concerning loving concern for each individual member of the church — even those "overtaken in sin."

1. *Galatians: A Commentary on Paul's Letter to the Churches in Galatia* (Philadelphia: Fortress, 1970) 54. See the detailed critique of Betz's interpretation in South, *Disciplinary Practices in Pauline Texts*, 117-28.

2. See Calvin J. Roetzel, *Judgment in the Community* (Leiden: E. J. Brill, 1972) 120-21, for an example.

3. J. E. Mignard, "Jewish and Christian Cultic Discipline to the Middle of the Second Century" (Unpublished Ph.D. dissertation, Boston University, 1966) 38.

4. Many of these same points apply to the discussion of I Corinthians 16:22, which is also subjected by many to the curse/death interpretation. See South, *Disciplinary Practices in Pauline Texts*, 133-36.

FOR THOUGHT AND DISCUSSION

1. State in your own words what Paul means by "flesh" and "Spirit" in Galatians 5:16 & 6:1.

2. Why do you think Paul does not specify the kind of sin which needs attention in Galatians 6:1?

3. Who are "the spiritual" in Galatians 6:1? How can you tell?

4. What might be the hazards of failing to "look to ourselves" in the exercise of church discipline? Do you know of instances where this was not done? What was the outcome?

5. How does the "curse/death" interpretation of Galatians 1:8-9 (and of I Corinthians 5:1-8) contradict the teachings of Jesus concerning church discipline?

"An important and sometimes neglected part of evangelism is to win Christians to Christianity, to disciple disciples, to win the *church* to Christ."

— F. D. Bruner, *Matthew*, Volume 2

DISCIPLINING THE DISORDERLY

(II THESSALONIANS 3:6-15)

John and Emily were intelligent, college-educated Christians with a lively family of six young children. In spite of their rather heavy family obligations, they tended to be a bit "quirky." John was an aspiring musician and song writer who preferred not to be burdened with an "ordinary" job so that he could be free to be creative and look for his big break. He would accept employment only temporarily and when forced to do so by necessity. Since Emily was totally occupied with the children and their numerous health problems, economic hardship was a way of life. Time and again John and Emily approached the church for help, and usually received what they requested. Although the elders and benevolence committee were somewhat put off by John's refusal to work steadily, the decision was usually made on the basis of the children; after all, it wasn't their fault that their parents were unwilling to put forth more effort to provide for them. So, over a period of years, the amount of help extended into multiple thousands of dollars. This continued until John deserted his family and Emily pulled away from the church, whose leaders finally concluded that their obligation to this difficult family had run its course. Unfortunately, by this time no one in the family was attending church or making any pretense of living a Christian life.

Similar stories have been repeated in churches more often than we care to admit. What do we do about people whose life-style isn't exactly "respectable," but who aren't committing any of the serious sins such as theft or adultery? And how far do we go in our compassion when such a situation continues and never seems to get any better? Do the Scriptures offer us any help, and is there any type of disciplinary action which might be useful in not only ending a frustrating and wasteful situation for the church, but in getting people more in line with God's will for their lives and perhaps saving them from even worse deviations?

"The Disorderly" at Thessalonica

A careful reading of II Thessalonians 3:6-15 reveals that such frustrating situations as John and Emily's are nothing new. The young church at Thessalonica had a problem with some members whose lives were "out of line," too. In what amounts to a major section of this brief letter, Paul gives some rather explicit instructions regarding them:

> But we command you, brothers, in the name of the Lord Jesus Christ, to hold yourselves aloof from every brother who conducts himself in a disorderly manner and not in keeping with the tradition which you received from us. For you yourselves know the necessity of imitating us, because we were not disorderly among you, nor did we eat bread from anyone without paying, but with toil and hardship we worked night and day in order not to burden any of you. Not that we do not have the right, but in order to give you in us an example to imitate. For when we were with you, we commanded you this: If anyone does not wish to work, then do not let him eat. For we hear that some among

you are conducting themselves in a disorderly manner, not busy but busybodies. Now we command and exhort such people in the Lord Jesus Christ to work quietly and eat their own bread. But the rest of you, brothers, do not become weary in the good you are doing. If anyone does not obey what we say by means of this letter, take notice of that person and do not associate with him, so that he will be put to shame. Do not regard him as an enemy, but admonish him as a brother.

(Author's Translation)

Comparing my translation above with some of the more recent ones (New International Version, Revised Standard Version, New Revised Standard Version), you notice right away a major difference: while most translations interpret the problem at Thessalonica as Christians "living in idleness," I have chosen to stay with the more literal rendering, "conducting themselves in a disorderly manner." Scholars and commentaries are about evenly divided over whether to translate in the more specific or the more general fashion. Some argue that the context, as brought out clearly in verses 8-10, demands that "living in idleness" is the correct translation. They would even go so far as to translate this way in I Thessalonians 5:14: "Admonish the idlers," even though there is nothing in the immediate context of I Thessalonians 5 to require it.

I have chosen the more literal and more general translation because the basic meaning of the word *ataktos* is not "idle" but "disorderly" or "undisciplined." Ancient writers used it to describe the disorderliness of matter prior to creation, of soldiers who were out of rank or shirking their duties, and even of irregular worship services.[1] While it is obvious that not working was a specific problem at Thessalonica, the translation "living in idleness" may obscure the reality that there was more at issue than mere idleness, and that idleness was only one manifestation of a larger problem. That larger problem seems to be the authority of the apostle Paul himself. The disorderliness of the Thessalonians lies in the fact that they are not living "in keeping with the tradition which you received from us" and in keeping with the example which the apostle and his associates had set while working among the believers there. This "tradition" apparently included instructions about Christian living as well as doctrine, and was backed up by the personal example of Paul and his friends. So in trying to correct the situation, he "commands" and "exhorts" "in the name of the Lord Jesus Christ" (vs. 6 and 12) and reminds them of an earlier "command" which they had been given but which they had not obeyed. Likewise, Paul makes it clear in verse 14 that further refusal to obey "what we say in this letter" is to be regarded as a serious offense. So the misconduct of the *ataktoi* (disorderly) at Thessalonica was a matter not only of not working but of disregard for established authority. Furthermore, verse 11 shows that not working was not the only manifestation of "disorderliness" among the Thessalonians. Some were "not busy but busybodies" (to preserve the word-play in Greek). They not only needed to work, but to "work quietly" (mind their own business?).[2]

Brotherly Avoidance

So what should the larger body of the church do in dealing with such disorderly members? Paul commands two concurrent courses of action: avoidance and continued warning. The command to avoid the disorderly comes in verses 6 and 14, where two rather general terms are used: "hold yourselves aloof from" (*stello*) and "do not associate with" (*me sunanamignymi*). The first term is one of general avoidance or withdrawal. The second means literally "not to be mingled with." These are not very specific instructions. We must ask further exactly what Paul had in mind. The other commanded course of action, continued warning, helps us interpret the first. Whatever might be involved in "avoiding" the disorderly, it obviously stops short of expelling them from the church's fellowship entirely, since it is assumed that there will be sufficient contact for warnings and admonitions to occur. Perhaps Paul had in mind generally avoiding the disorderly in social settings, but continuing to associate with them at church. Verse 10 implies that the disorderly remain within the community of believers but are denied some of the privileges of membership — specifically, the right to sit at the common table where believers shared their food.[3] Regardless of the specific actions involved, "Do not let him eat" must surely exclude providing material support for disorderly members.

This brings up two important points: First, we have in this verse a specific example of what was said in an earlier chapter about discipline and its necessary context, a close-knit Christian fellowship. Verse 10 raises many interesting questions about early Christian table-fellowship, but one thing is plain: the fellowship and mutual dependence were close enough that the larger body could deprive the disorderly of the right to eat! Does this help us understand why *our* disciplinary efforts are frequently so ineffective? Is it not simply a reflection of our puny "fellowship"? As I. H. Marshall has well put it, "One may suspect. . . that the nature of the Christian community has changed. Discipline is possible and necessary within a fairly compact, closely-related group, but this may not be so in the rather loose association typical of many modern congregations."[4] Are today's churches anything like the close-knit and mutually-dependent Thessalonian church, or are we merely a "rather loose association" of people who happen to meet for worship in the same location? The answer will tell us much about our ability to discipline effectively. This may seem like an argument against the possibility of such discipline in today's church, since there is seldom this kind of material/financial dependence. But it does occur, as in John and Emily's case, and it reinforces the earlier point that before we can strengthen our discipline, we must strengthen our fellowship.

The other significant point to observe is that verse 10 has to do with discipline *within the congregation*. It is not about our "benevolence" toward those outside, although the text is usually quoted and applied in these situations. When needy people come to the church for help, we ought not to apply verse 10 across the board. Some are genuinely unable to help themselves, and to require that they rake leaves or wash windows before we will help them can be cruel. Our help may come in the form of a job for those who are able to perform one, but II Thessalonians 3:10 ought not to be our primary rule of thumb in dealing with people in need. On the other hand, we probably ought to employ it more than we do in the case of Christians, such as John and Emily, who habitually rely upon the church to do for them what they could do for themselves. Ironically, we are sometimes more "benevolent" toward people who need discipline than toward those who need benevolence! Although, as explained above, II Thessalonians 3:6-15 does not deal exclusively with idleness, but rather with "disorderliness" in general, it certainly provides us with practical guidance in dealing with "John and Emily" situations.

"Warn Him As a Brother"

As in all the texts we have examined so far, Paul's concern for the Thessalonians was not only the health and purity of the church, but the salvation of individual Christians — even the erring ones. He continues to refer to such an offender as a "brother" (vs. 6 and 15). And he cautions the Thessalonians not to "regard him as an enemy," but to "admonish him as a brother." He still belongs to Christ. Although his life is out of harmony with Christ's will, the situation does not yet call for more drastic action (such as treating him "as a Gentile or tax collector").[5]

This raises an important question: Why does Paul not speak more specifically about what he wants the church to do in regard to "the disorderly"? Why the general terms of avoidance and warning, rather than more specific instructions, such as those found in Matthew 18:15-17 and I Corinthians 5:5? One answer may be that "it is difficult, if not impossible, to frame precise rules when dealing with personal relationships."[6] Even in situations requiring discipline, people are still people, and hard-and-fast rules are seldom helpful. It would seem that Paul has deliberately left his instructions ambiguous within the broad outlines of avoidance and brotherly admonition. The point is to achieve the desired results: maintaining the church's health and purity and the offender's salvation. Paul leaves it open to the church to decide exactly what might be required in the case at hand to accomplish the goal. It is important to note that Paul does not here, as he did not in Galatians 6:1, repeat the "steps" outlined in Matthew 18:15-17, although he could have done so easily enough. Instead, he leaves the church free to take whatever action might be necessary to reclaim the particular offender and to protect the church at large. If a relatively informal course of warning and admonition would accomplish the purpose, there would be no need to go further, since the goal is restoration and not punishment. Or, more stringent warnings and more complete avoidance might be brought to bear if lesser measures failed. Paul does not "command" the specific steps to be taken; what he does command is that the church do what it can to remedy the situation.

But what, practically speaking, are the options open to a congregation in dealing with its disorderly members? What exactly does brotherly avoidance coupled with continued warning look like, and how does it work? What specifically might a church do in order to correct the disorderly short of a total withdrawal of fellowship? The possibilities are as varied as the situations which might prompt them. One might be, as suggested above, continued association in worship but limited association on a social level. However, since in all congregations there are members who have little or no "outside" association with other believers, the purposes of such limitations would have to be made explicit — that is, that the person was being avoided for a specific reason and for redemptive purposes. This necessity is reinforced by Paul's speaking to the entire Thessalonian congregation about such action, not to only a few, and certainly not only to the elders or other leaders. In such a situation, all encounters, whether at worship or in other settings, could be used as occasions for warning and admonition. The point would be not to allow the disorderly brother or sister the enjoyment of Christian fellowship without the consequences of such fellowship, that is, mutual responsibility. If every encounter with fellow believers resulted in admonitions and warnings, the disorderly would soon be forced to decide how important fellowship is and whether they want it to continue.

In cases such as John and Emily's, where the disorderliness involves an over-dependence on the church for some type of support, whether material or emotional, Paul's words are immediately relevant: the refusal to correct misbehavior should result in having that support cut off. An example of non-material support would be a person who continually seeks "counseling" from church leaders but refuses to accept their guidance in matters of spiritual discipline. Such people can become a constant drain on the time and emotional energy of church leaders. If they refuse to do what they can to help themselves, the situation should not be allowed to continue. If this type of action seems harsh or unloving, we should ask ourselves what those Thessalonians thought who showed up at the common table or the church pantry, only to be denied access! Just as in raising a child, the truly unloving course would be to allow the disorderly to experience no consequences at all for their actions, thus reinforcing sinful behavior which could result in the loss of their relationship with God altogether. In circumstances where such action seems called for, we must trust the wisdom of God that it will be more effective in redeeming the disorderly than a "softer" approach which may on the surface seem to be "more loving," but which actually may be motivated by its being easier for us. No one ever said that discipline would or should be easy.

The important fact to note at this point, as we will see, is that church discipline cannot be reduced to a sequence of "steps" to be applied in all cases. This is not what Paul did, and churches in our own time have often blundered by not recognizing the built-in flexibility of the divine instructions. In dealing with erring members, we are faced with a wide range of options, within the broad guidelines found in this text and others, and we should be ready to use them all, if necessary, to reclaim one of Christ's lost sheep or to caution one just beginning to stray. We can go astray in many ways. Thank God, that he provides numerous means for returning us to his fold!

1. For the specific ancient references, see South, *Disciplinary Practices in Pauline Texts*, 162.

2. The traditional understanding of the idleness at Thessalonica is that it was the result of the mistaken belief that Jesus was to return very soon; thus the normal routines of life were meaningless — including working for a living. This is a plausible reconstruction of the situation, since both Thessalonian letters indicate that misunderstandings of the coming of Jesus were part of the problem at Thessalonica. However, nothing in either letter connects these misunderstandings with the problem of idleness. It may be that the two problems were unrelated: many people refuse to work who have no particular convictions about the coming of the Lord. (For a series of persuasive arguments against the traditional understanding of the Thessalonian idleness, see B. N. Kaye, "Eschatology and Ethics in 1 and 2 Thessalonians," *Novum Testamentum* 17 [1975] 47-57.)

3. Although some see v. 10 as a reference to the Lord's Supper, it seems probable that Paul's reference is more general. The connection between not working and not eating argues for a more mundane understanding of "eating." Plus, refusing someone the right to eat the communion would seem to involve a more complete exclusion from the community of believers.

4. *1 and 2 Thessalonians* (Grand Rapids: Eerdmans, 1983) 229.

5. The Stoic philosopher and Roman emperor Marcus Aurelius likewise advises the avoidance of those who behave roughly and rudely, and like Paul, says not to treat them as enemies. However, he gives no counsel concerning reforming the offenders. "The Stoic individualism and the Christian sense of obligation towards a brother are thrown into sharp contrast. . . " (James Moffatt, "2 Thessalonians iii. 14, 15," *Expository Times* 21 [1909-10] 328).

6. Marshall, 228.

FOR THOUGHT AND DISCUSSION

1. Have you known of "John and Emily" situations in churches where you have worshiped? What was the eventual outcome? Do you think discipline could have made a difference?

2. Why do you think churches are usually so slow to apply disciplinary principles in "John and Emily" situations?

3. What are some specific ways in which Christians might practice "avoidance" in dealing with "disorderly" members?

4. In what ways do Paul's instructions to the Thessalonians presume a close-knit fellowship of believers?

5. What should we conclude from the fact that Paul gives only rather general instructions about how to treat disorderly members? How does this compare to the practice described in the scenario in the Introduction?

"Cheap grace is the preaching of forgiveness without requiring repentance, baptism without church discipline, Communion without confession, absolution without personal confession."

— Dietrich Bonhoeffer, *The Cost of Discipleship*

DRASTIC DISCIPLINE: INCEST AT CORINTH

(I CORINTHIANS 5:1-8)

I Corinthians 5:1-8 is one of the few New Testament texts on discipline which deals not only with a specific sin, but with a specific *case* of sin. It is therefore of particular interest in any study of church discipline. But because it deals with a specific case, and a drastic one at that, we must keep in mind that it does not constitute a pattern for church discipline in general. Rather, it supplies guidance for dealing with extreme cases of moral deviation among Christians. The texts studied so far have dealt with "sin" more generally, and it is from them that we should draw our basic principles of action such as concern for the salvation of the offender, dealing with sin as privately as possible, attempting to restore, and handling each situation individually and not according to some hard-and-fast scheme of disciplinary "steps." In other words, it is important that we realize that not every case of discipline should involve "delivering someone to Satan"!

Incest at Corinth

The Corinthian situation was a drastic one indeed, because it had wide-ranging consequences not only for the man committing the sin but for the entire congregation. Paul's relationship with the Corinthian church was stormy, to say the least. There were numerous challenges to his authority as an apostle of Christ, especially when he spoke authoritatively in dealing with some of the illegitimate behavior and theology in the church. But rather than retreating, Paul speaks very directly about the problems at hand, perhaps partly to test their willingness to be obedient. His confrontation concerning the incestuous man is very direct:

> Sexual immorality is actually reported among you, even such immorality as is not (permitted) among pagans, to the extent that someone has his father's wife. And you are puffed up! Should you not have mourned instead, so that the one who has done this deed might be removed from your midst? For I, being absent in body but present in spirit, have already, as one who is present, judged the one who has done this. When you are assembled in the name of the Lord Jesus and my spirit (is there) with the power of our Lord Jesus, deliver that man to Satan for the destruction of the flesh, in order that the spirit may be saved in the day of the Lord. Your boasting is not good. Do you not know that just a small amount of leaven ferments the entire lump of dough? Remove the old leaven so that you may be new dough, just as you are unleavened. For our Passover lamb, Christ, has been sacrificed. To this end let us celebrate the feast, not with the old leaven which is the leaven of malice and evil, but with the unleavened bread of sincerity and truth.
>
> (Author's Translation)

Although some specific aspects of the situation at Corinth

are unknown, its general outline is clear. Someone in the church is involved in an ongoing[1] sexual liaison with "his father's wife." The unusual expression "his father's wife" virtually assures that the woman is not his mother, since that would have been easy to state, and there is little question that Paul would have done so had that been the case. It is unclear whether the man's father is still living or is divorced from his wife. Since Paul shows no particular concern about the woman's conduct or how the church should respond to her, it seems safe to assume that she is not a Christian.

It is not so surprising that a case of sexual immorality might occur in a Christian congregation. After all, it was a feature of the pagan environment in which churches such as that at Corinth existed, as attested by the frequent warnings against it in the New Testament (Gal. 5:18-21, Eph. 5:3-5, Col. 3:5-10). But the case of immorality at Corinth was especially shocking because it was "such as is not (permitted) among pagans." In my translation the word "permitted" is in parentheses because there is no corresponding verb in Greek. Paul literally says, "such immorality as is not among pagans." But he surely does not mean that such cases never *occurred* among pagans,[2] but rather that such was neither lawful nor acceptable. In fact, such liaisons were forbidden by Roman law and were looked upon with revulsion in Greek and Roman society alike. But the condemnations and allegations found in ancient sources prove that such practices existed in pagan society.[3] But even there it did not exist with approval, and how alarming that it should be tolerated in the church of Christ!

Not only is the presence of such immorality shocking to Paul, but also the church's attitude toward it: "And you are puffed up!"[4] But why would any church be arrogant about having such sin occurring among its members? Apparently there was an air of broadmindedness prevailing at Corinth that could not be offended by even so repugnant a situation. It may well be that the Corinthians felt that their superior "spirituality" (4:8) was vast enough to tolerate such things, and they were proud of it.

It's not unusual, even in our own time, to see churches react against legalism and a judgmental spirit by becoming over-tolerant and proud of their superior understanding, as opposed to their less-enlightened brothers. Such arrogance is highly dangerous, as the Corinthian excess illustrates. They should have been in mourning over the wickedness in their midst and their failure to deal with it, but pride had overruled repentance. No wonder Paul was dismayed!

The Demand for Drastic Measures

Paul unhesitatingly calls for drastic measures, not only to deal with the incestuous man's sin, but also to correct the church's arrogant spirit.

He states first of all that the one who has done such a thing must be "removed from your midst" (v. 2), and then outlines the prescribed action more specifically in verses 3-5. Paul's reaction to immorality is in sharp contrast to that of the Corinthians, as brought out by the Greek construction of verse 3, where "For I. . ." stands at the beginning of the sentence, in contrast to "And you. . ." at the beginning of verse 2. Although not physically present, Paul is present "in spirit,"[5] and has already judged the situation just as if he were there. There is no question what the church must do. Meeting in solemn assembly, they are to "deliver that man to Satan."

But what did Paul mean by this strange command? Not surprisingly, it has been the subject of much speculation and debate. The expression "to deliver to Satan" is unusual and occurs elsewhere in the New Testament only in I Timothy 1:20, where Paul refers to Hymenaeus and Alexander, "whom I have delivered to Satan that they may learn not to blaspheme." The verb *paradounai* means "to deliver" or "hand over" and suggests that Paul intends the offender to be given over in some sense to the power of Satan. He doesn't pause to elaborate but moves on to express the intended result of this "handing over": "for the destruction of the flesh, so that the spirit may be saved in the day of the Lord." In spite of the many scholars who claim that what Paul had in mind was the use of a curse ("deliver to Satan") expected to result in death ("the destruction of the flesh"), the context makes it obvious that Paul is talking about "putting him out of the church," or, as it is usually stated, "disfellowshipping."[6]

This conclusion is justified by the following observations:

(1) Paul has already said that the incestuous man should be "removed from your midst" (v. 2).

(2) In verses 6-8 Paul draws heavily on the Passover theme, particularly with reference to the Feast of Unleavened Bread just prior to Passover, when the Israelites removed all "old leaven" from their homes (see, e. g., Ex. 12:15). "A little leaven leavens the whole lump" — the influence of the incestuous man in their midst will inevitably be pervasive. Others may imitate his boldness and even those who do not will be negatively affected by such uncleanness in their midst. So, just as Israel "put away" the old leaven, they must remove him from their midst. They are already late with this: "Our Passover lamb, Christ, has been sacrificed." The old leaven was to be removed *before* the slaying of the Passover lambs. Christ has already died for our sins. The time is long past for his church to be tolerating such "leaven" in their midst.[7]

(3) Verses 9-13 speak clearly of *not associating with* immoral people. Paul had addressed this problem in an earlier letter (which we do not have), and now clarifies that he was speaking specifically of not associating with those who call themselves our "brothers" yet live like pagans. They are not even to "eat with such a person," which probably refers both to the Lord's Supper and to "secular" meals. In other words, such people should no longer be admitted to the church's fellowship on any basis.

(4) Verse 13 contains a commandment frequently found in Deuteronomy: "Drive out the wicked person from among you."[8] These words emphatically instructed Israel to remove evil from their midst; likewise, Paul uses these words to encourage the

Corinthians to do the same thing.

This is clearly a more complete and more severe action than what Paul had commanded the Thessalonians. In this case there is no "warning him as a brother" or continual admonitions to do better. Nor do we find Paul recommending a three-step process of going to the sinner with a progressively wider circle of witnesses. This is not to say that Paul has no concern for the spiritual welfare of the incestuous man: the ultimate goal is "so that the spirit may be saved in the day of the Lord." But the situation is a dangerous one, and it requires serious measures. When someone's house is on fire, we do not politely knock at the door! There is imminent danger, not only to the man himself but to the church, which has already been impacted negatively by his actions, whether they recognize it or not. There are times when the church must act, and act quickly, in order to minimize the damage done by a flagrantly sinning member. However, we are usually quite slow to act, even in such drastic cases as Paul outlines here. Our great fear is that we not act "too hastily" in dealing with such situations. It is hard to imagine Paul giving such a precaution to the Corinthians! In reality, our more usual error is the failure to act at all, or else to drag the whole process out to such lengths that irreparable and unnecessary damage is done while we try to decide "what to do." As stated at the beginning of this chapter, the action prescribed here is not for every situation. But it *is* for cases of blatant and dangerous sin, and we ought not to hesitate to employ it when warranted. Delivering someone to Satan is indeed "radical surgery," but there are times when, in the spiritual realm as in the physical, such surgery is necessary. It is impossible to calculate the damage which has been done by our failures (or slowness) to act in such situations, not only within congregations but by defaming the church in the eyes of the community.

But how do we determine when a situation calls for such drastic action? To some extent, this must be left to the judgment of the church, under the guidance of its leaders. Paul offers us some specific help in verse 11 where he names some additional sins which might require severe measures for correction: sexual immorality, greed, idolatry, slander, drunkenness, and theft. This list should probably be regarded as representative and not exhaustive, that is, not *all* of the sins which might demand "delivery to Satan," but the *types* of sins. It should be noted that some in this list, such as greed and slander, are not ones which usually show up on our lists of "terrible" sins. But they can betray deep-seated spiritual problems and can cause serious destruction within a congregation. Oftentimes the greatest havoc is wreaked in congregations, not by people who are flagrantly immoral, but by those with the ungodly attitudes of bitterness, hostility, jealousy, and selfish ambition. Yet these are almost never disciplined. Another guideline is that provided by Jesus in Matthew 18:15-17. *Any* sin in which a fellow-Christian stubbornly persists after being admonished repeatedly must eventually be dealt with by complete avoidance. Apparently Paul does not go through the "steps" outlined in Matthew 18, not because he did not know them, but because the Corinthian situation was already well-known to all and was too dangerous not to deal with speedily.

Objections

Two objections are frequently raised against the practice of withdrawing the church's fellowship, even in cases of severe and persistent sin. One is the charge that such an action is unloving, that the only hope of reforming the offender is continued patience and a "non-judgmental" attitude toward his/her behavior. But such a response betrays a decidedly un-Biblical understanding of what "love" means and a lack of seriousness about the consequences of sin. Real love will refuse to sit by and watch a loved one commit sins which will inevitably result in eternal condemnation without doing *everything* possible to prevent it. In the very next chapter, Paul warns: "Do not be deceived; neither the immoral, nor idolaters, nor adulterers, nor sexual perverts, nor thieves, nor the greedy, nor drunkards, nor revilers, nor robbers will inherit the kingdom of God" (6:9-10). As in the physical realm, so in the spiritual: when death is imminent, severe and painful measures may be unpleasant but are in no way unloving. The real love-question is, do we love one another enough to take whatever action is necessary to bring about repentance?

The second objection is, how will withdrawing fellowship from someone help the situation? Will the sinning Christian not simply become more hardened and turn completely away from the church? Going back to the text, although Paul does not state it, his assumption seems to be that delivering someone to Satan will hopefully induce repentance. This will in turn lead to the salvation of the person's spirit on the day of the Lord. As in Jesus' instructions in Matthew 18:15-17, the hope seems to be that the shock of being ostracized by the entire body of believers will cause the offender to realize what he/she has lost in the present and what will be lost in eternity. Although this is Paul's stated goal for the disciplinary action, there is certainly no guarantee of its effectiveness; the sinning Christian may, in fact, become hardened in sin. In that case the salvation of the individual becomes secondary to the preservation of the church as a whole. The "old leaven" must be removed before it spoils the "whole lump." There is an element of trust involved here. Since these are the instructions which we have in the Scriptures, we must trust that in God's wisdom such measures will be effective when prayerfully and humbly employed. The refusal to engage in such stringent disciplinary measures, even when clearly called for in Scripture, is a sign of our mistrust of the word which God has given us — the only word we have for divine guidance. Perhaps we need to do less speculating about its wisdom, and as obedient children find out what God can and will do through our conformity to his word.

Withdrawal, Holiness, and Fellowship

By now the connections between the withdrawal of the church's fellowship and the larger concerns of holiness and congregational fellowship ought to be obvious. Without holiness no one will see the Lord, and discipline — even drastic discipline — is essential to preserving our holiness. Paul's appeals to the leaven/Passover themes brings this out clearly. But again, such measures can only be effective where fellowship is vital and real, in churches where fellowship, once withdrawn, would be sorely missed, and where brothers and sisters are genuinely pained to witness sin in each other's lives and are unwilling to ignore it. In such churches, where love prevails and holiness before God is of primary concern, even the most severe forms of Godly discipline can be effective.

APPENDIX B

A CRITIQUE OF THE "CURSE/DEATH" INTERPRETATION

In our discussion of Galatians 1:8-9 (Appendix A), I explained that a significant number of New Testament scholars maintain that early Christian discipline involved the use of curses which were expected to result in the death of the offender, as in many ancient Greek and Jewish curse formulas. According to this view, the primary goal of church discipline was simply to remove troublesome members who compromised the church's standards and identity. Enough has been said already to demonstrate the inadequacy of this interpretation. But because I Corinthians 5:5 is so frequently interpreted in this manner, it deserves further discussion. The curse/death interpretation of this verse maintains that "delivery to Satan" involved placing the offender under a curse and that the "destruction of the flesh" signifies physical death, resulting in eventual salvation.[9] In other words, the sinner's death in some way makes salvation possible.

This view is to be rejected for the following reasons:[10]

(1) As noted in Appendix A, the Greek and Jewish curse formulas on which this practice is supposedly based are not genuine parallels to I Corinthians 5:5.

(2) Acts 5:1-11 and I Corinthians 11:30 are not parallel to I Corinthians 5:5. These two texts, often cited in support of the curse/death interpretation, speak of people receiving "capital punishment" for spiritual offenses. But in both of these texts the deaths are punitive and not redemptive, and neither of them says anything about any act of the assembled church, which Paul requires in I Corinthians 5. The deaths which occurred were the direct act of God and in no way were the result of anyone being "cursed."

(3) The only New Testament verbal parallel to "deliver to Satan" excludes the idea of death. In I Timothy 1:20 Paul states that he had delivered Hymenaeus and Alexander to Satan "that they may learn not to blaspheme." They were not expected to die, but to learn something from being disciplined.

(4) The curse/death view is against Paul's usual use of the flesh/spirit contrast. The curse/death view demands that "destruction of the flesh" means physical death, leading to the salvation of the soul. But when Paul contrasts "flesh" and "spirit," he is usually referring to different attitudes and orientations of life — not to a contrast between soul and body. (See Gal. 3:3, 5:13, 16-26, 6:8; Rom. 8:3-18.)

(5) As noted in the discussion above, the context itself explains the meaning of "delivery to Satan": exclusion from fellowship (vs. 2b, 9-13).

(6) The curse/death view cannot account for the fact that the offender is to be delivered to Satan "so that the spirit may be saved in the day of the Lord." It is totally inconsistent with all New Testament teaching to believe that one's own death could somehow "atone" for sins. Only the death of Christ has atoning power.

1. The present infinitive (*echein*) indicates the on-going nature of the offense.

2. This is so even though many translations suggest otherwise: "and such fornication as is not so much as named among the Gentiles" (KJV); "and of a kind that is not found even among pagans" (RSV, NRSV); "and of a kind that does not occur even among pagans" (NIV); "and immorality of such a kind as does not exist even among the Gentiles" (NASB). Such translations are justifiable only if Paul is understood as saying that such immorality does not exist *with approval* from Gentile society in general. But it seems better simply to supply a more realistic verb; in our translation, "permitted."

3. For examples from various Greek and Roman sources, see South, *Disciplinary Practices in Pauline Texts*, 29-30.

4. "Puffed up" is an expression which occurs often in this letter, as an indication of the spirit of arrogance which infected the Corinthian church. Note the allegations of arrogance in chapters 1-4, 8, and 13.

5. It is difficult to know exactly what Paul means by his "spiritual presence" in vs. 3 and 4. He certainly implies more than just, "I'll be thinking about you," and seems somehow to see himself as "with them" spiritually. Certainly the letter itself conveyed a sense of Paul's "apostolic presence" as it was read in the assembly. See II Cor. 10:10-11, where Paul emphasizes that the dichotomy between his bodily presence and his "letter presence," as expressed by his opponents, is a false one.

6. "Excommunication" is not an inaccurate term for what Paul is talking about, but because of its "loaded" meaning in various religious contexts, I have chosen to avoid it. But we should remember that "disfellowship" is no more Biblical a term than "excommunicate."

7. For a further discussion of the imagery of leaven in Paul's letters, see C. L. Mitton, "New Wine in Old Wineskins: IV. Leaven," *Expository Times* 84 (1972/73) 339-43, and J. K. Howard, "'Christ Our Passover': A Study of the Passover-Exodus Theme in I Corinthians," *Evangelical Quarterly* 41 (1969) 97-108.

8. Deut. 13:6, 17:12, 19:13, 21:21, 22:21, 22:22, 22:24, 24:7.

9. For examples of this view, see C. T. Craig, "The First Epistle to the Corinthians, *The Interpreter's Bible* (New York and Nashville: Abingdon, 1953), Vol. X, 62; Hans Conzelmann, *A Commentary on the First Epistle to the Corinthians* (Philadelphia: Fortress, 1975) 97; W. F. Orr and J. A. Walther, *The Anchor Bible*: I Corinthians (Garden City, New York: Doubleday, 1976) 186. Some believe that the incestuous man was expected to die, but do not connect this with a curse: C. K. Barrett, *The First Epistle to the Corinthians* (New York: Harper & Row, 1968) 126-27; F. F. Bruce, *1 and 2 Corinthians*

(Grand Rapids: Eerdmans, 1971) 54-55.

10. For a fuller discussion of the curse/death interpretation and its refutation, see South, *Disciplinary Practices in Pauline Texts*, 38-65. Also, J. T. South, "A Critique of the 'Curse/Death' Interpretation of I Corinthians 5.1-8," *New Testament Studies*, Vol. 39 No. 4, October, 1993, 539-61.

FOR THOUGHT AND DISCUSSION

1. Why should we be cautious about using I Corinthians 5 as a "normative" text for church discipline?

2. What does Paul mean by "delivering someone to Satan"? Why do you think he uses such dramatic terminology? Why don't we use it?

3. How does delivering someone to Satan differ from the kind of avoidance taught in II Thessalonians 3?

4. Why doesn't Paul tell the Corinthians to "go through the steps" as outlined in Matthew 18:15-17? Are there times when this is not required or advisable? Why or why not?

5. Why does Paul include an "attitude" sin such as "greed" in his list of those requiring discipline? Have you ever known anyone to be disciplined for such a sin?

"Humanity is never so beautiful as when praying for forgiveness or else forgiving another."

— Jean Paul Richter

WHEN A BROTHER NEEDS FORGIVENESS

(II CORINTHIANS 2:5-11)

Bill caught all of us off guard that Sunday morning when he walked in the back door of the auditorium. I remember my first thought as if it were yesterday: "What does *he* want?" I later learned that most others in the small congregation felt the same way. It had been only a few months since Bill had boldly announced that he was leaving his wife and two lovely children for another woman with whom he had been carrying on an illicit relationship for several years. Despite all pleas from the church and his family, he moved in with the other woman, right before the eyes of the watching community. There was only one course of action open to the church, and we took it, not in a hostile way, but with fear and trembling. In a meeting of the entire congregation, after discussing the Bible's teaching on discipline, we agreed that we must withdraw our fellowship from Bill, and did so the following Sunday.

Still, there was a great deal of anger in our hearts toward Bill. It was all so senseless, so unnecessary, so tragic. And he was so callous about it! So when he walked in that Sunday morning, he didn't find a group of people who were in a very forgiving mood.

At the close of the sermon, we found out what he wanted. He walked to the front of the auditorium during the invitation song, sat down on the front pew, and began to confess tearfully what a fool he had been. He had had everything, but threw it all away. He acknowledged everything that we and his family had tried to tell him months earlier. And he begged for God's forgiveness — and ours.

I'd like to report that we were overwhelmed with sympathy and compassion for our fallen brother, but it wasn't that easy. We accepted his statement of confession, but it took awhile to even begin to really forgive him. We had become frozen in our anger toward him, so that when he responded to God's discipline and to his own foolishness, we weren't ready to receive him back. After all, the damage had already been done. Besides, none of us had thought beyond the process of discipline. Once our fellowship had been withdrawn, that was the end of it. Or so we thought.

This story highlights an important truth about the church's fellowship, especially as it relates to the drastic breaches in that fellowship that sometimes inevitably occur: *Disciplining an offending brother or sister is never an end in itself*. As we have seen in Matthew 18:15-17, the goal is restoration and forgiveness — not discipline. Discipline is merely the necessary means to achieve that goal. And whenever we enter into the process of discipline, whether individually or congregationally, we should already be thinking about the goal and looking forward to the healing of the broken relationship. Of course, we have no way of knowing in advance what will be the outcome of our efforts, but if we plan for the worst, it is unlikely that we will experience the best. The attitude that we must discipline, even though "it won't do any good," is much like evangelizing with the same assumption. We severely lessen the chances that it *will* "do any good," and even if it does prove effective, we will be ill-prepared to capitalize on the positive results. Disaster is likely to result anyway. *It is imperative that the church learn to discipline lovingly and to expect positive results from our efforts*. Otherwise we will continue to experience the disastrous results that all too often accompany discipline in the church. As Jesus taught so plainly in Matthew 18, the goal of lovingly confronting a sinning Christian is to "gain your brother." If our goal is less than that, it is not likely that our efforts will be tempered with the right spirit that will result in someone's returning to the Lord and his people.

A Penitent Sinner at Corinth

The church in Corinth was confronted with a similar situation to the one I described earlier. After considerable conflict and confusion, the church had expelled from its fellowship a man who had been sexually involved with his father's wife (I Cor. 5:1-13; see Chapter 9). As a result, the man had repented, and now Paul writes to instruct the church what to do. That he had to write to them about this suggests that they, too, were having difficulty responding appropriately to a penitent brother. Paul's instructions are as follows:

> But if anyone has caused grief, he has not caused it to me, but to some extent — though I don't wish to be harsh — to all of you. For such a person this punishment by the majority is sufficient. But now in place of that you must forgive and comfort him, lest he be overwhelmed by excessive grief. Therefore I urge you to confirm your love for him. This is why I wrote, that I might know your character — that is, whether you are obedient in all things. Anyone whom you forgive of something, I forgive also. For indeed what I have forgiven, if I have forgiven anything, has been on your behalf in the presence of Christ, so that we may not be defrauded by Satan. For we are not ignorant of his schemes.
>
> (II Corinthians 2:5-11, Author's Translation)

Paul begins the body of II Corinthians with a defense of his travel plans, specifically with an explanation of his failure to visit Corinth as expected (1:12ff). Apparently some were pointing to this failure as evidence of his unreliability and lack of integrity (1:15-22). Beginning in 1:23, however, Paul explains that his failure to come had another motive altogether. He had wished to spare the Corinthians further pain by avoiding what he anticipated would be an unpleasant confrontation with them.

It is at this point (2:1-4) that we learn that there had already been an unpleasant and, in Paul's mind, unproductive confrontation with the Corinthians, which he had followed with a letter of stinging rebuke. These have come to be known as the "painful visit" and the "sorrowful letter." A later reference to this letter in II Corinthians 7:8 shows that it was not only written out of anguish, but that it likewise had produced considerable grief in the community when they read it. It becomes evident in 2:5-11 that the chief source of this friction between Paul and the Corinthians was a certain individual who had in some way caused offense. It is obvious from Paul's comments that this particular issue played a crucial role in the defense of his ministry (chaps. 1-7), and thus was a central concern of the entire letter. Paul speaks of the incident as well known to his readers. The man and his offense require no further identification.

II Corinthians 2:5-11

One of the interesting aspects of this text is that it is the only one which speaks about discipline *after the fact*. The church has already carried out Paul's instructions toward the offender, and their efforts have produced the desired result. What now?

Apparently in the Corinthians' minds, the offense which precipitated the "painful visit" and the "sorrowful letter" was primarily against Paul himself, but he seeks to dispel this notion by pointing out that the "pain" (or, "sadness") was actually experienced by the entire church. He downplays the personal element in order to focus on the real problem: the injury to the church. In highlighting the broader effect of the offense, Paul shows sensitivity not to make the offender's guilt weigh any more heavily than necessary. The term *epibarein* ("to weigh down," "to burden") is peculiar to Paul in the New Testament[1] and is always metaphorical for a burden placed upon another. Paul does not wish to over-burden the guilty party (who remains unnamed throughout), but he wants the church to see that there is more involved here than a mere personal affront. Perhaps Paul knows that they have been reluctant, as churches sometimes are, to recognize the whole affair as a communal problem. This failure to recognize the damage suffered by the church is part of the problem.

In verse 6 Paul pronounces the disciplinary action taken by the community as *hikanos*, "sufficient." This could mean either that it had gone on long enough, or that it had been severe enough. The former is more likely, since Paul says to end it, not alter it. The action is described as "this punishment."[2] The use of this term, coupled with Paul's plea for its reversal, strongly implies a formal act on the part of the church. The expression "by the majority" raises the possibility that the action was not unanimous, and that there may have been a dissident minority. 6:1-13 indicates that there was still a pocket of resistance to Paul and his authority.

Because the punishment is "sufficient," another course of action is now called for (v. 7). The offender now requires both forgiveness and comfort in order to prevent his being "overwhelmed" (or perhaps, "drowned" — *katapino*) in an excess of grief over his sin. Paul is concerned that the discipline not be carried too far, that it be effective but not vindictive. Its purpose has been accomplished and, if continued, it could become destructive. Most likely Paul is afraid that the offender may be so overwhelmed by his grief and by the continued rebuke of the church that he will abandon his faith altogether. Note Paul's obvious concern for the sinner's welfare. Even though he has been guilty of a serious sin and has brought considerable trouble to the congregation, he is not to be "pruned" or cast off in order to purify the church. The goal, once again, is to regain him if at all possible.

Paul encourages the Corinthians to extend to the penitent offender a formal expression of their love (and forgiveness — vs. 7 and 10). The verb *kyrosai* ("to confirm," "to ratify") denotes the confirmation of a sale or the ratification of an appointment to office. Paul uses it again in Galatians 3:15 of the ratification of someone's will. He is apparently calling for an *act* of reaffirmation of the community's love for the offender as an expression of his continued place among them. There must be no doubt that the offender has regained his place among his fellow believers.

"This is why I wrote" (v. 9) is undoubtedly another reference to the "sorrowful letter" mentioned in verse 3 rather than to I Corinthians. As painful as that letter had been to write, it evidently had the desired effect. Its purpose was to serve as a test of their character, particularly of their willingness to be obedient "in all things."

In verse 10 Paul shows his willingness to concur in the church's judgment regarding the penitent man. If they forgive, Paul forgives him. Once again he downplays the personal aspect of the offense by inserting "if I have forgiven anything," and by insisting that his forgiveness of the offender has not been intended to satisfy any personal requirement on his part, but is "on your behalf in the presence of Christ."

The first clause of verse 11 continues the thought of verse 10: Paul is willing to forgive whomever they forgive in order to prevent Satan from "defrauding"[3] the church. If both the church and Paul do not forgive the offender, Satan may cheat them. It is serious business to fail to forgive when the time comes.

Steps to Restoring Fellowship

This important episode in the life of the Corinthian congregation impresses upon us what all is involved in fully restoring someone to fellowship following discipline by the church.

1. *Forgiveness*. Now that the disciplinary action of the church has had its desired effect, Paul tells the church that "in place of that you must forgive. . . him" (v. 7). Paul has already forgiven him (v. 10), and now the church must follow his lead. His tone of urgency and exhortation suggests that he expected forgiveness not to come easily. And frequently it does not, as in our difficulty in forgiving Bill. Often in cases requiring the discipline of the church, there is considerable anger and hard feelings. The process may be long and involved and create a measure of dissension within the congregation, as it had at Corinth. In the course of all this, it's easy to lose sight of the goal: to restore, not to punish. It's true that Paul refers to the church's discipline as "punishment" in verse 6, but he says that the punishment is "sufficient." Once repentance has occurred, the time for punishment is over. The withholding of fellowship is only a step in the process, not its ultimate goal. Now it's time for forgiveness. If we find that hard, we need only think of all of the times that God has graciously forgiven us, and we don't deserve it any more or less than does our erring brother or sister.

2. *Comfort*. Once an erring Christian has repented, the process is not over for him or her any more than it is for the congregation. Even though forgiven by God and by the church, there's still the shame and embarrassment of it all which must be dealt with. So part of the restoration process is extending comfort as well as forgiveness (v. 7). This might be accomplished in several ways. One would be the reassurance that sinning and being disciplined does not make the penitent offender different from other Christians. After all, Hebrews 12 reminds us that "the Lord disciplines those whom He loves." We are all in the process of being disciplined by God, in order "that we may share His holiness" (Heb. 12:10). That's why Paul cautions those who engage in attempting to restore others to do so in a spirit of gentleness, "looking to yourself, lest you, too, be tempted" (Gal. 6:1). This is in no way intended to make light of the penitent's offense; it simply recognizes that we all are equally in need of God's grace. And what greater comfort could there be than to be reminded that the God who calls for our discipline does so

because of his gracious love! Restored sinners need to be reassured that God isn't "finished" with them simply because they have "blown it." After all, the Bible is filled with the stories of people — such as Moses, David, and Peter — who "blew it" and yet were still loved and valued by God.

3. *Confirmation of Love.* "Therefore I urge you to confirm your love for him" (v. 8). It is often said that one's penitence should be as public as one's sin; that is, if one sins publicly, a public confession is in order. Paul seems to suggest something similar in the case of confirmation of love: the church should make its expression of love as public as its discipline! In II Corinthians 2 he's apparently calling for a specific *act* of reaffirmation of the church's love, as suggested by the use of the aorist infinitive *kyrosai* ("confirm," "ratify"; New English Bible: "I urge you therefore to assure him of your love for him by a formal act."). Alfred Plummer paraphrases verse 10 in this way: "I therefore implore you to leave him no longer in suspense, but at once, by some formal act, put into execution, not any sentence of further punishment, but the renewal of your love for him."[4] By whatever means necessary, both formally as a collective body and individually, we must make it clear that our love for the penitent offender is as strong as ever. If done in the right spirit, discipline in no way will have diminished our love, and we must be prepared to show it.

Consequences of Failing to Restore Fellowship

Paul's admonition to the Corinthians also gives ample warning of the serious consequences which can result if a church aborts the disciplinary process by failing to forgive and fully restore the sinner to fellowship.

1. *The penitent sinner may be lost due to overwhelming guilt and grief.* Paul urges forgiveness and comfort of the offender, "lest he be overwhelmed by excessive grief" (v. 7). If discipline

is carried beyond the point necessary to induce repentance, it becomes destructive. Penitent sinners who return to the body of Christ seeking restoration and forgiveness generally experience an enormous degree of guilt and shame. If they are not quickly confirmed by their brothers and sisters, they may abandon the faith entirely. Paul speaks of being overwhelmed by "excessive" grief, that is, more grief than necessary to induce repentance. As noted above, the word translated "overwhelmed" (*katapino*) means to be swallowed up or drowned. The image of a penitent sinner drowning in excessive grief while the church stands by and refuses to offer its forgiveness and comfort is one which no congregation can bear to contemplate.

2. *The church is guilty of disobedience.* According to verse 9, Paul had earlier written to the Corinthians regarding this matter, to see "whether you are obedient in all things." Initially his concern was their obedience in disciplining the immoral brother, something which they were extremely reluctant to do (I Cor. 5:1-5). Now that they have complied, he wants them to be equally obedient in expressing their love and forgiveness. We must learn that extending forgiveness is not an option depending on how we happen to feel. When Paul instructs the Corinthians to forgive, he reflects the teachings of Jesus, who taught his followers that forgiveness is required of all who wish to be known as his disciples. Just after Jesus taught his disciples not to "write off" those who sin against them, but to go to them personally and seek to regain them, Peter asked, "Lord, how often shall my brother sin against me, and I forgive him? As many as seven times?" Jesus' reply must have shocked Peter: "I do not say to you seven times, but seventy times seven" (Matt. 18:21-22). He followed this with the parable of the unmerciful servant and the declaration, "So also my heavenly Father will do to every one of you, if you do not forgive your brother from your heart" (18:35). The church is never at liberty to think that we've "done our duty" by disciplining the erring when we are unwilling to perform the equal "duty" of forgiveness.

3. *Satan succeeds in defrauding the church.* In verse 11 Paul explains that forgiveness and restoration are necessary, "so that

we may not be defrauded by Satan. For we are not ignorant of his schemes." Even in the act of disciplining the erring, the church must never forget that Satan is always "scheming" against us, seeking ways to turn even holy things to our destruction. If we discipline the erring and then refuse to reinstate them fully, we play right into his hands! Paul says we are "defrauded" by him. How? For one thing, whenever discipline occurs without forgiveness and reconciliation, Satan has an opportunity to promote tension and division among us and to rob us of an opportunity for healing and growth. Even worse, however, he robs us of the soul of a brother or sister. What a tragedy, for someone to be penitent and at the point of restoration, only to be rebuffed by a lack of loving forgiveness, and then be drowned in grief and give up on the faith! We must be painfully aware that the failure to act mercifully at this critical point in someone's life may result in Satan getting just what he wants.

At that crucial moment in a Christian's life when sin gives way to godly sorrow, the church must respond with forgiveness, comfort, and confirmation of our love. Only then will we realize the benefits of godly discipline, both for our penitent brother or sister and for the body as a whole.

APPENDIX C

I CORINTHIANS 5 AND II CORINTHIANS 2: THE SAME, OR SEPARATE INCIDENTS?

Until the beginning of this century, scholars were virtually unanimous in identifying the incestuous man in I Corinthians 5 with the man needing forgiveness in II Corinthians 2. Since the turn of the century, however, the roster of those rejecting this view has become formidable and their rejection is emphatic.[5] Those who follow the traditional view are few indeed.[6] But weighing the arguments on both sides, there still seem to be good reasons for identifying the offender to be disciplined in I

Corinthians 5 with the one to be forgiven in II Corinthians 2.

(1) On the basis of verses 5 and 10, most commentators conclude that the situation in II Corinthians 2 involves some personal insult to Paul concerning his authority as an apostle, not the situation of immorality discussed in I Corinthians 5. However, it should be noted that in these verses Paul actually attempts to correct the Corinthians' assumption that he is the one who has been wronged. At the risk of further burdening the now-penitent offender, he emphasizes the corporate nature of the injury and denies that he is the injured party (v. 5). And, although he offers his personal forgiveness in verse 10, he downplays its significance and focuses on the forgiveness which needs to be expressed by the church collectively. This corresponds well with the idea that the incestuous man in I Corinthians 5 was "leavening the whole lump" by his behavior. The case of incest was, indeed, a "test case" of Paul's authority, and it may have been that the incestuous man took the lead in rejecting Paul during his "painful visit" (II Cor. 2:1), but the real damage was to the church itself.

(2) Beginning with Tertullian[7] in the early third century, scholars have raised the argument that Paul could not have so roundly condemned the man in I Corinthians 5 and then counseled his forgiveness in II Corinthians 2. But this points to a fundamental misunderstanding of the purpose of the discipline commanded in I Corinthians 5. It was not merely for the offender's punishment — certainly not for his death, as many maintain — but "that his spirit may be saved in the day of the Lord Jesus." II Corinthians 2:5-11 is an indication of the effectiveness of such action. Paul's fear in II Corinthians 2 that Satan might gain an advantage over or defraud the community is easily understood as taking the disciplinary action too far. The offender was delivered to Satan in order to motivate him to repentance and restoration, not to destroy him

(3) Another frequent argument against the identification of the two offenders is that no sexual offense is mentioned in II Corinthians 2. While this is obviously true, it is also true that no offense of *any* kind is specifically mentioned, not even one which

constitutes a particular affront to Paul.

(4) While there are certainly some differences between the two texts, such as the involvement of Satan in the discipline of I Corinthians 5 and the fear of his activity in II Corinthians 2, we should not overlook that there are also some striking similarities. Both refer to Satan's activity, both invoke the name of Jesus in solemn oaths, both discuss communal discipline (yet to be accomplished in I Corinthians 5, almost completed in II Corinthians 2), and both require the church to act in obedience to apostolic authority.

(5) In spite of the considerable arguments which have been made against the identification of the two offenders, there are two generally-overlooked questions which seem to support the idea. The first is, could Paul have written as he did in II Corinthians 2 unless the problem of the incestuous man had been satisfactorily resolved since his writing of I Corinthians 5? It is difficult to imagine him writing in anything like a conciliatory tone if that issue had gone unresolved. Admittedly there is still tension between Paul and the Corinthians when he writes II Corinthians, but there is a strong note of conciliation as well (1:3-7, 3:3, 7:1-16). Could Paul have been proud, comforted, and joyful over a community that had failed to acknowledge his authority and was still puffed up with arrogance in spite of the outrageous sin in their midst? It hardly seems likely. The second question is, if the problem had been resolved prior to the writing of II Corinthians, would Paul have written to them again without mentioning it? Would he have simply ignored the fact that so crucial an issue had been resolved? Would he not rather have expressed his great relief and joy for the resolution of the problem in much the same terms that we find in II Corinthians? If II Corinthians 2 does not refer to the same incident as I Corinthians 5, it would seem necessary to postulate a resolution to the problem and an acknowledgment from Paul which took place in the interim between I and II Corinthians.

Thoughtful consideration of these two questions, as well as of the arguments presented above, would seem to tip the balance in favor of the identification of the two. I conclude, then, that when Paul wrote concerning the man in need of forgiveness in II Corinthians 2, he was acknowledging the church's repentance of its first refusal (which is implied, if not stated, in v. 9) to discipline the incestuous man, and encouraging them to receive him back on the basis of his repentance.

1. The other occurrences are I Thess. 2:9 and II Thess. 3:8.

2. C. K. Barrett, *A Commentary on the Second Epistle to the Corinthians* (New York: Harper & Row, 1973) 90, objects to the translation of *epitimia* as "punishment," but this still seems the most natural translation.

3. This translation is preferable to RSV's "gaining the advantage over us" and NIV's "outwit us," because it fits better with Paul's *pleonekteo* ("take advantage of," "outwit," "defraud," "cheat") in II Cor. 7:2 and 12:17-18. Satan may do the very thing which some had accused Paul of doing — "defrauding" the church.

4. *A Critical and Exegetical Commentary on the Second Epistle of St. Paul to the Corinthians* (New York: Scribner's, 1915) 52.

5. These include, to name only a few, C. K. Barrett, *Essays on Paul* (Philadelphia: Westminster, 1982); M. J. Harris, *The Expositor's Bible Commentary: 2 Corinthians* (Grand Rapids: Zondervan, 1976); Rudolph Bultmann, *The Second Letter to the Corinthians* (Minneapolis: Augsburg, 1985; German edition, 1976); R. P. Martin, *Word Biblical Commentary: 2 Corinthians* (Waco, Texas: Word, 1986); R. V. G. Tasker, *The Second Epistle of Paul to the Corinthians* (Grand Rapids: Eerdmans, 1958); F. F. Bruce, *1 and 2 Corinthians* (Grand Rapids: Eerdmans, 1971); and James Thompson, *The Second Letter of Paul to the Corinthians* (Austin: Sweet, 1970).

6. See, for example, G. W. H. Lampe, "Church Discipline and the Interpretation of the Epistle to the Corinthians" in *Christian History and Interpretation* (Cambridge: University Press, 1967); P. E. Hughes, *Paul's Second Epistle to the Corinthians* (Grand Rapids: Eerdmans, 1962); A. M. G. Stephenson, "A Defense of the Integrity of 2 Corinthians," in *The Authorship and Integrity of the New Testament* (London: S. P. C. K., 1965). Ernest Best, *Second Corinthians* (Atlanta: John Knox, 1987) is among the few who remain neutral on the question.

7. *On Modesty* 13.

FOR THOUGHT AND DISCUSSION

I. How does the expectation of positive results from our disciplinary efforts affect the outcome?

2. Comparing II Corinthians 2 to I Corinthians 5, do you agree or disagree that they both discuss the same case of discipline? Why or why not? Does your conclusion affect your understanding of the need for forgiveness of penitent offenders?

3. What might a congregation do to "make the restoration as public as the discipline"?

4. Why are members of a congregation sometimes angry toward someone who has been disciplined? Is such anger justified? Why or why not?

5. Why is it important to remember Satan's schemes as we go about the practice of church discipline?

"Diotrephes is the father of a long line of sons who have not learned to distinguish between love for Christ and His Church and love for their own place in it."

— Anonymous

DISCIPLINING THE DOMINEERING

(III JOHN 9-10, TITUS 3:10-11)

Lyle was an intelligent man, a Christian college graduate, well-versed in the Bible, and a deacon in the church. These might all sound like favorable qualities, but Lyle used them in a very manipulative fashion. Most of the people in the blue-collar congregation, including the elders, were intimidated by his knowledge and intellect. So when he spoke, everyone felt compelled to listen. And he spoke often. Every time someone did something he didn't like, Lyle would complain to the elders and confront the "offender" with an accusation of "liberalism," which basically meant any position or action with which he disagreed (even though he himself held some very peculiar and questionable beliefs). This had gone on for years, and the church had settled into a pattern of little activity for fear of arousing Lyle's ire. Any time he objected to something, it was stopped. As a result, the congregation was being dominated by one man's opinions on just about every matter. The situation was stifling and deadening in its effect, but no one seemed to know what to do about it, and many didn't even recognize what was happening. So, to keep the peace, no one said or did anything. Finally, a young preacher came along who didn't know any better, and he openly challenged Lyle on several occasions. This gave the elders courage, and they, too, began to resist his domineering ways and to refuse to allow him to control the church. Finding that he could no longer bluster his way over others, Lyle very shortly left for another congregation, only to begin the same pattern of behavior all over again.

In trying to think of an example of such domination, it was difficult to select just one. Unfortunately, the church never seems to lack its "Lyles" — people with controlling personalities who care more about getting their own way than about the welfare of the church, or even than the will of God! Such people bully, threaten, sow seeds of discord, spread rumors, make accusations, and complain, all with a single goal in mind: getting their way. Sadly, because we are not accustomed to the practice of church discipline in other matters, we seldom know how to deal with a "Lyle." And so these cantankerous and destructive people go on year after year, dominating the churches they attend, stifling good works, exhausting the leadership, intimidating good people into silence, and generally depressing the church and forming it into their own image. To borrow (out of context) a statement from James, "My brothers, this ought not to be so!" (James 3:10b). It is not right to sit idly by and watch any man or woman dominate the Lord's body, particularly since the Scriptures give us ample guidance about how to deal with a "Lyle." It is time that we wake up and acknowledge that much of our "keeping the peace" in the face of someone like Lyle is in reality a direct disobedience to Biblical teachings

In this chapter we will examine a text from John and one from Paul which speak directly to the problem of dealing with domineering people. These people are highly dangerous, and it is not surprising that both John and Paul deal with them in a very straightforward manner and encourage us to do likewise.

III John 9-10: Dealing With Diotrephes

We cannot be certain who "Gaius" was (III John 1) to whom John addressed his third letter, or where the church of which he was a member was located. But we know that they had a "Lyle" to deal with. In his very personal note to Gaius, John says that he has written also to the church, but that someone named Diotrephes was opposing his teaching and creating considerable trouble in the congregation:

> I wrote something to the church, but the would-be leader Diotrephes refuses to acknowledge us. So if I come, I will bring up the things he is doing, bringing ridiculous charges against us with malicious words. And as if that were not enough, he refuses to welcome the brothers himself and forbids those who want to do so and casts them out of the church.
>
> (Author's Translation)

The problem evidently centered about the need for churches to welcome traveling missionaries, a service which Gaius had performed in a commendable manner (vs. 5-8). John had written to the entire congregation about this, but Diotrephes refused such instruction and prevented others from fulfilling their duty and even "disfellowshiped" those who defied him! His reasons? He "loves to put himself first," to put it literally.[1] In other words, he wanted to have his way, even if it meant putting an obstacle in the way of Christian charity and the spreading of the gospel. He also was not above blackening the reputation of John, perhaps by means of rumor and back-stabbing accusation. John did not intend to let this pass; he would deal with Diotrephes personally when he came (v. 10). We might wish that John had been more specific about what he intended to do, but the important point to notice is that he has no intention of letting Diotrephes get away with his words and actions — not because they were personally painful to John, but because Diotrephes, like Lyle, was standing in the way of the progress of the gospel.

But notice the characteristics and activities of Diotrephes, which are frequently true of the domineering:

1. He had his own agenda for the church, even though it meant hindering the spread of the gospel.

2. He refused to acknowledge any authority but his own.

3. He used malicious words as a weapon against those who stood up to him.

4. He put a stop to the good works of others because of his own rebellious spirit.

5. He wanted to "de-church" everyone who refused to agree with him.

Sounds a lot like Lyle, doesn't he! Not only does John intend to deal with him, but he also encourages Gaius not to be swayed by him, but rather to imitate the good works of people such as Demetrius (vs. 11-12). The worst thing we can do with a "Diotrephes" (or a "Lyle") is to allow him to stop us from doing the good which we would otherwise do! Such people can be notoriously difficult to stand up to, but it can and must be done.

Titus 3:10-11:
De-Fusing the Divisive

Just as John wrote to Gaius in his local congregational setting, so Paul writes to Titus in the context of his work among the churches on the island of Crete (Tit. 1:5). It was a difficult work, and the life of the churches was marred by false teaching (1:9-10ff) and a quarrelsome spirit (3:9). Concerning the latter, Paul urges Titus to "avoid stupid controversies, genealogies, dissensions, and quarrels over the law, for they are unprofitable and futile." Numerous suggestions have been made as to the nature of these controversial issues,[2] but regardless of their specific content, Paul labels them as "stupid" and counsels Titus to "avoid" them.[3] As for those who persist in promoting such controversies, he says,

> Reject a divisive person after a first and second warning, knowing that such a person is perverted and is sinning and stands self-condemned.
>
> (Author's Translation)

A legitimate question here is whether the people Titus had to deal with were merely creating problems over their opinions on various matters, or were false teachers who promoted doctrines which were contrary to the gospel and to apostolic teaching. Some would draw a distinction between someone like Diotrephes, who was "merely opinionated" and a "false teacher," who clearly espouses something contrary to revealed truth. In many congregations, a "Lyle" would be tolerated indefinitely, but someone who believes something considered to be "unscriptural" would be quickly branded, if not ostracized. But this text makes us question whether such a distinction is warranted. The problem in this passage seems to be not with any specific doctrine which is being contradicted or a falsehood being promoted, but with the general attitude and resulting divisiveness of those who enjoy controversies and the quarrels which so often accompany them.

Paul labels this kind of person as a *hairetikos*, which I have translated as "a divisive person." The King James Version used the word "heretick," which prejudices the discussion toward someone who promotes doctrinal deviation, which is what the word "heretic" has come to mean. The Greek word is actually an adjective used as a noun, and denotes someone who is part of a sect or faction (such as the "sects" of the Pharisees and Sadducess — Acts 5:17, 15:5 — or even of the Nazarenes — Acts 24:5). It is concerned not so much with the truth or falsehood of the view being held as with the reality of creating division among bodies of people.[4] This may be the result of teaching something contrary to Scripture, or it may simply involve the opinionated views, persistently advocated, by a Diotrephes or a Lyle! Notice that in Titus 3:9 nothing specifically is said about false teachings, but only about the stupidity and controversial nature of the quarrels being carried on. This is not to suggest that false teaching may not be involved. Given the overall context of the letter, it very likely was.[5] But Paul's concern is not so much doctrinal as practical: the discussions "are unprofitable and futile." A person who would promote such things must be dealt with decisively because he/she poses a serious threat to the unity and overall health of the church.

So, what are we to do with a "Lyle"? Paul says to give him two warnings and then "reject" him. Because he's still a brother in Christ, we must try to turn him away from his sinful behavior; therefore he must be warned of the consequences of his actions and attitude. But because of the danger he poses to the well-being of the church, the "warning process" must not go on forever. Two warnings are the maximum allowed![6] After that, rejection. It may be that the words of Jesus about going to a sinning brother require the first and second warning, but it should be noted that Paul does not require exactly the same procedure, perhaps because of the imminent danger posed by one who would, for the sake of his/her own opinions, threaten the unity of the church.

But what is involved in such a "rejection"? The verb *paraiteomai* is rather vague and means generally "to decline," "reject," or "refuse." At the least it would suggest staying away from and refusing to be influenced by anyone creating division. At the most it might mean a formal withdrawal of the church's fellowship. We can well imagine John coming to the congregation where Diotrephes was asserting himself and warning the church to stay away from him. Or, we can equally imagine him encouraging the church to disfellowship him entirely, depending on his further attitude and actions after being warned of his sin. Once again, we see that Paul does not feel compelled to spell out for the church how far its discipline must go. He is mostly concerned with "damage control" where such people are concerned, whether that requires individual avoidance or congregational action. But under no circumstances can a "Lyle" simply be ignored or catered to.

The reason that such decisive action is called for, rather than a period of going repeatedly to the factious person, lies not only in the nature of his/her actions, but in the nature of such people themselves: "knowing that such a person is perverted and is sinning and stands self-condemned" (v. 11). To take delight in creating dissension and to be so determined to have one's own way is not only sinful but also "perverted." Unfortunately, there are people who take a perverse delight in controversy. Usually disguising their warped motives as a quest for "doctrinal soundness," they are quick to engage in a fight over almost anything, just as Paul suggests in verse 9. Even when warned by the church at large or by its leaders, they will not stop. Frequently, as in the case of Diotrephes, they will respond to correction or opposition with slander and malicious words rather than face up to their own sin. Paul's sad verdict applies to such people today as much as it did in his own time: they stand "self-condemned." Their very refusal to consider the peace of the church or the feelings and opinions of others, and their willingness to engage in unwarranted verbal assaults, reveals their true character. "Lyles" seldom repent.

The words of Paul and John are a warning to us all. The "Lyles" among us must be recognized for what they are and dealt with accordingly. Otherwise, disaster is sure to result. If the "Lyles" are allowed to have their way, the church will languish under their domination and fail to do the good works which God has laid before it. Or, it may become so embroiled in silly arguments about phony "issues" that all of its energies are sapped and it has nothing of substance to say to the unbelieving community around it. And such disunity may well lead to division, at great cost to all involved. But godly discipline, lovingly but boldly administered, can prevent all of this and enable the church to move on unhindered by the pettiness of a domineering brother or sister. Genuine fellowship demands that we not ignore the destructive potential of someone like Lyle. And our quest for God's holiness requires that we press on in our service to him, without the unholy influence and stifling arrogance of misguided people.

1. "The language suggests a self-promoted demagogue rather than a constitutional *presbyteros* or *episkopos*" (F. F. Bruce, *The Epistles of John* [Grand Rapids: Eerdmans, 1970] 152). B. F. Westcott labels this section of the letter, "the temporary triumph of ambition" (*The Epistles of St. John* [Grand Rapids: Eerdmans edition 1966] 239). He adds, "There is nothing to indicate that Diotrephes held false opinions: his ambition only is blamed" (240).

2. See, for example, the suggestions in G. W. Knight III, *The Pastoral Epistles* (Grand Rapids: Eerdmans, 1992) and Donald Guthrie, *The Pastoral Epistles* (Grand Rapids: Eerdmans, 1957).

3. Literally, "go around" them (*perihistemi*).

4. This is reflected in most recent translations: "divisive" (NIV) ; "factious" (NASB, RSV) ; "contentious" (REB) ; "any one who causes divisions" (NRSV).

5. This is assumed by most commentators. See, for example, Knight (353-54), Guthrie (208), and William Hendriksen, *New Testament Commentary: Exposition of the Pastoral Epistles* (Grand Rapids: Baker, 1957) 395. Although Guthrie adds, "The Greek word *hairetikos* translated *heretick* does not mean what the word 'heretic' means today. It designates one whom Simpson describes as an opinionative propagandist who promotes dissension by his pertinacity'. In later times the word acquired a more technical meaning of 'one who holds false doctrine'" (208).

6. The RSV rendering "once or twice" might suggest that there is an option of giving only a single warning. However, Paul's words literally read "after a first and second warning."

FOR THOUGHT AND DISCUSSION

1. Have you ever personally known a "Lyle"? What was his impact on the congregation as a whole?

2. Why do you think churches are so often intimidated and reluctant to deal with a "Lyle"?

3. In what ways can people sometimes be divisive without actually teaching false doctrine? Give specific examples.

4. How are people such as those discussed in this chapter dealt with in your congregation?

5. Why do people such as Lyle/Diotrephes seldom repent? How does this serve as a warning to the rest of us?

"There is a kind of peace which can be had at the cost of evading all issues, refusing all decisions, shutting the eyes to things that are crying out to be dealt with, a peace which comes of a lethargic inactivity and an avoidance of all decisive action. The Christian must ever remember that the peace of God is not the peace which has submitted to the world, but the peace which has overcome the world."

— William Barclay, *The Letter to the Romans*

WATCHING OUT FOR FALSE TEACHERS

(ROMANS 16:17-18)

Acts 20:17ff describes a particularly poignant meeting between Paul and his long-time friends, the elders of the church at Ephesus. Believing that he will never see them again (vs. 37-38), Paul warns them to

> Take heed to yourselves and to all the flock, in which the Holy Spirit has made you overseers, to care for the church of God which he obtained with the blood of his own Son. I know that after my departure fierce wolves will come in among you, not sparing the flock; and from among your own selves will arise men speaking perverse things, to draw away the disciples after them. Therefore be alert....

Over and over again the New Testament puts us on guard

against the presence of false teaching, whether it arises, as in the case of the Ephesians, "from among your own selves" or as an invasion from outside forces. Jesus himself gave such warnings (Matt. 24:4ff), and the threat of false teaching is never very far from the minds of the inspired writers of the various letters.[1] In spite of these warnings, churches are often caught off guard when false teaching arises and are therefore unprepared to deal with it in a constructive and helpful manner. As a result, unhealthy (the literal meaning of "unsound") teaching leads to unhealthy living and unhealthy churches, and possibly even to spiritual destruction.

Because of the seriousness of this situation, the Scriptures give us not only warnings about false teachers, but also instructions about dealing with them, in order to prevent them from wreaking havoc on the body of Christ. We need to acquaint ourselves and our congregations with these instructions *before the fact*, so that when circumstances require it, we are prepared to exercise the needed discipline in an effective manner.

Romans 16:17-18: Rejecting Falsehood and Opting for Truth

But I encourage you, brothers, to watch out for those who cause dissensions and hindrances in opposition to the teaching which you learned; turn away from them. For such people do not serve our Lord Christ; they serve their own bellies. And by means of smooth talk and flattery they are deceiving the hearts of those who don't know any better.

(Author's Translation)

Paul had never been to Rome at the time he wrote his famous letter to the church in that city (Rom. 1:13-15). But that didn't mean that he didn't know anyone in the church there. To the contrary, the final chapter of the letter indicates that he knew a surprisingly large number of people. He spends the first 16 verses of Romans 16 giving greetings and commendations to a large number of friends and acquaintances, something which he normally doesn't do in his letters. Apparently he does so here because he did not himself begin the Roman church and can safely greet everyone he knows without fear of hurting anyone's feelings, as might have happened in a church which he had begun himself.[2] But regardless of his reasons, the important thing is that all of those greeted are people who have been faithful to the apostolic message as Paul preached it.

Although most translations do not indicate it, verse 17 actually begins with the word "but," as in my translation above.[3] False teachers are now being deliberately excluded from the greeting extended to the faithful in verses 1-16. Although the word *koinonia* is not used, fellowship is the general topic of verses 3-23. Those who are fellow-believers and fellow-workers are to be greeted in the Lord. But those who disrupt that unity by their teachings are to receive a different kind of treatment entirely.

That these offenders are false teachers of some sort, and not merely opinionated or domineering people (see Chapter 11), is made abundantly clear by Paul's description of them: "those who cause dissensions and hindrances *in opposition to the teaching which you learned*." While we cannot determine with any certainty what their "heresy" was or even who they were, it is obvious that they were teaching things which were in conflict with the gospel message which the Romans had received. Their motive is made plain in verse 18: they do not serve Christ, but their "own appetites," and they are not above using flattery and deceit in order to gain an audience for their views. This is an important insight into the motive behind much false teaching: while it may supposedly stem from a desire to "be Scriptural," it may actually reflect a perverse desire for attention or an effort to gain a personal following. This seems to be reflected in Paul's warning to the Ephesian elders (Acts 20:30: "to draw away the disciples after them"). Not all "doctrinal" disputes are really about doctrine!

So what should a church do when confronted by such people? Paul uses two words to designate the required actions.

The first is *skopeo*, which I have translated "watch out for," and which signifies critical observation of someone. It is not an inherently negative term,[4] as shown by its use in Philippians 3:17: "Brothers, join in imitating me, and *take note* of those who so live as you have an example in us." This verse is in a very real sense the positive counterpart of Romans 16:17. Just as the Romans must "watch out for" false teachers, so the Philippians are advised to "take note of" positive examples of Christian living and teaching. The King James translation of *skopeo* as "mark" has led to the unfortunate practice of "branding" as false teachers people with whom we disagree about something, regardless of how trivial, which in turn is sometimes used as an excuse for slandering them far and wide, often without even confronting them personally. It's clear from Paul's language and from the context that such practices are *not* what he is recommending. Even though "watching out for" a false teacher might involve a public identification of that person before the congregation, there is absolutely no warrant in this verse for the irresponsible labeling of a brother or sister to the brotherhood at large.

But Paul does not counsel us merely to observe troublesome teachers: he also says to "turn away from them." I have chosen "turn away from" rather than the usual "avoid" to translate the verb *ekklino* because it implies a deliberate rejection of a person (Rom. 16:17), of evil conduct (I Pet. 3:11), or of righteous conduct (Rom. 3:12). Practically speaking, such a rejection might involve nothing more than my personally refusing to talk to someone about his "pet" views. Or, it might go further and take the form of a formal action by the congregation as a whole, depending on the false teacher's persistence. Turning away from such a person could be either a warning to the whole church not to be influenced by such a person's views, or even a complete withdrawal of fellowship, if he/she is a member of the congregation and persists in spreading falsehood. Again, by not specifying exactly the action to be taken, Paul has left us free to tailor the action to suit the need.

Notice that Paul says nothing about giving two warnings, as in Titus 3:10-11, or about going to the false teacher privately and then in the company of witnesses, as in Matthew 18:15-17. In fact, he says nothing at all about seeking to restore the false teacher. This seems somewhat contradictory to his words in II Timothy 2:24-26:

> And a servant of the Lord is not required to fight but to be kind to all, to be capable of teaching, to be forbearing, to correct opponents with gentleness, since God may grant to them repentance leading to knowledge of the truth and that they may come to their senses and escape the devil's snare, having been captured by him to do his will.
>
> (Author's Translation)

Likewise, these softer words stand in sharp contrast to Philippians 3:2, where Paul warns against the influence of "Judaizers," people who taught that Gentiles must be circumcised in order to be saved. "Look out for the dogs, look out for the evil-doers, look out for the mutilators!" How do we reconcile these texts? The most likely explanation is that the false teachers which Paul has in view in Romans 16:17 and Philippians 3:2 are not part of the church, but trouble-makers who may be expected to come (or have already come) in from outside.[5] On the other hand, the "opponents" of II Timothy 2 are most likely Christians who have strayed into error, "having been captured by him (Satan) to do his will." Staunch defense is required in the one instance, gentle teaching in the other. Comparing II Timothy 2:24-26 with Titus 3:10-11, there is no reason why the "first and second warnings" which Paul requires to be given to the divisive individual (apparently a fellow-Christian) cannot be done with the gentle and forbearing spirit required by II Timothy 2. The point of Titus 3 seems to be not to be *too* forbearing in the case of individuals whose perversity of mind can be of serious danger to the peace of the church. Again, the controlling principle is, suit the action to the need.[6]

Our Common Responsibility

Notice that in writing to the Romans, Paul speaks in the second person plural in instructing them to watch out for and turn away from false teachers. It's *everyone's* responsibility to be discerning about the teachings which we hear and to avoid those who would lead us astray. Likewise, John cautions all of his readers not to believe every spirit, but to "test the spirits to see whether they are of God" (I Jn. 4:1). In the "Letters to the Seven Churches" found in Revelation 2-3, the risen Christ scolds two of the churches (Pergamum [2:12-17] and Thyatira [2:18-29]) for tolerating people in their midst who promoted false teaching and false living. Only a minority of the people in those churches were guilty of false teaching, but the entire membership of both churches is held responsible for their failure to act to correct the situation. But the Ephesian church, in spite of its other problems, has "tested those who call themselves apostles but are not, and found them to be false" (Rev. 2:2). "He who has an ear, let him hear what the Spirit says to the churches!"

Unfortunately, we are often too much like the churches of Pergamum and Thyatira. There's a widespread tendency to turn a blind eye and a deaf ear toward such deviations, rather than acting to confront them. Even when disturbed by false teachings in their midst, Christians often will sit silently by and wonder why "someone" doesn't do something? Why is this? For one thing, it's much easier not to "rock the boat" than to raise the alarm about someone's teaching or behavior. Also, in our drive to "reach the community," we sometimes go overboard in trying to appeal to worldly-minded people who might be repulsed if they overheard us dealing seriously with false doctrine and conduct. Likewise, there are always within our churches those who follow the "cult of broad-mindedness," which insists that we must tolerate almost anything in order not to be thought "narrow-minded." Another reason for failing to discipline false teachers is that they are sometimes influential people within the congregation[7] due to their wealth, position of leadership, or long-standing membership. Sadly, one of the most common reasons why we do not discipline false teachers is that so many Christians are so Biblically illiterate that they don't recognize many erroneous teachings as false. I have known of several situations where false views of the nature of Christ were being openly taught, and virtually no one in the congregation even realized it!

But there is likewise a very legitimate concern which often paralyzes us in the face of false teaching: the fear of developing a "head-hunter" mentality. We have all seen the ugliness of churches and individuals who major in finding fault in others and "labeling" them as false teachers, and no one in his or her right mind would want to become part of such a perverse activity. So how do we go about fulfilling the Bible's instructions without falling into the trap of becoming over-critical and nit-picky? Allow me to make some suggestions:

1. *Recognize that not all beliefs are of equal importance.* When Paul wrote to the Corinthians about the resurrection of the dead, he identified as of "first importance" such things as the death, burial, and resurrection of Jesus (I Cor. 15:3ff), indicating that there is a difference between these and things of "second importance." Likewise, the "seven ones" of Ephesians 4:4-6 are truths which all believers presumably must hold in common: one body, one Spirit, one hope, one Lord, one faith, one baptism, and one God. But there are other matters which do not fall into any of these categories, and on these there will always be disagreements among believers. When the New Testament speaks about "false teaching," the context almost always indicates that the concern is with the central truths of the gospel, not with more peripheral matters. This ought to give us a strong clue about which matters should concern us in a disciplinary way and which should not. Unfortunately, sometimes we lose perspective on such matters and are more ready to discipline (or "label") someone with whom we disagree over a peripheral matter than we are to confront a genuinely false teaching. We have all seen situations in which more "heat" was generated over a matter such as whether to eat in the church building than over

erroneous teaching on the nature of Christ!

2. *Remember that the Scriptures allow room for "private opinion."* In Romans 14-15 Paul deals with conflicts between two factions which he describes as the "weak" and the "strong." Such issues as dietary scruples and the observance of certain "special" days were points of contention. Interestingly, Paul does not attempt to determine who is "right" and who is "wrong" in these matters. What he is more concerned about is *how they treat each other* as they attempt to resolve their disputes. He nowhere indicates that they must decide right and wrong on every issue. And if someone happens to hold a view which is potentially divisive or harmful if expressed, he is allowed to "keep it between himself and God." As long as someone is not creating a problem over some personal point of view, there is no need for discipline. On the other hand, even a peripheral matter can become divisive and dangerous if it is pressed unnecessarily, and may then call for the discipline of the church (see Chapter 11).

3. *Observe the congregational context of all church discipline.* Because the church exists as local bodies of believers, discipline must be exercised on that level. So far in our study of discipline, we have not seen a single instance where anyone is instructed to "discipline" by spreading information about a brother or sister brotherhood-wide. There are cases where individual avoidance is called for, and others where congregation-wide action is necessary. We might even find it necessary to give warning to a church which is being invaded by someone who has created "dissensions and hindrances" in other places. But we are nowhere authorized to become "doctrine police" for the church at large. Such efforts may be well-intentioned, but they are seriously misguided. If we keep our discipline within the family (the local church), it will go a long way toward keeping us from becoming brotherhood busy-bodies and gossips. Besides, who among us doesn't have enough to do in seeing to the needs of our own congregation, without trying to "police" the activities of those in others! Those who are always critical of what is going on elsewhere seldom are doing a very good job at home.

4. *Remember that discipline should begin with personal*

confrontation. The idea that as long as someone's sin is "doctrinal" in nature we are free to publicize it to whomever we wish is thoroughly un-Biblical. Even in cases where we suspect blatant false teaching by a brother or sister, we are still obligated to go to the person and confront him/her in an effort to restore. Again, keeping discipline within the context of the local church makes this workable and effective. It also makes us less likely to criticize the beliefs of another without knowing what we are talking about.

Somewhere between the two extremes of tolerating any teaching which comes along and making an issue of every disagreement there lies a narrow ground of responsible spiritual discernment. It is that ground which the Scriptures call us to occupy. The concerns of our faith are simply too great for us to fail to "test the spirits," but the consequences of being over-zealous about doctrinal purity are equally drastic for the peace and unity of the church. Our common faith is the basis of our fellowship together, and we must guard that foundation at all costs, while at the same time remembering that those with whom we disagree will often be our brothers and sisters. Likewise, our identity as God's holy people requires that we be true to his word, but also that we not injure the body unnecessarily in the process. The narrow ground may be difficult to hold, but it is there where we must live.

1. E. g., Rom. 3:8; I Cor. 15:l2ff; Gal. 1:8-9, 3:1; Eph. 5:6ff; Phil. 3:2ff; Col. 2:8ff; II Thess. 2:lff; I Tim. 1:3ff, 4:lff; II Tim. 4:lff; Tit. 1:l0ff; II Pet. 2:lff, 3:3ff; I Jn. 2:l8ff, 4:lff; II Jn. 9-11; Jude 8ff, etc.

2. The only other letter in which Paul calls several people by name is Colossians, also written to a church which Paul did not begin and had never visited.

3. RSV and NIV leave the *de* ("but") untranslated. NASB has "Now I urge you, brethren. . . ."

4. *Skopeo* is used outside the New Testament to describe the critical observation of the judge, the philosopher, and the historian. For the variety of uses of this word and its compound forms, see E. Fuchs, *"skopeo,"*

Theological Dictionary of the New Testament, ed. by G. Friedrich and G. W. Bromiley (Grand Rapids: Eerdmans, 1971) Vol. 7, 414-15.

5. On the basis of v.19, most commentators favor the view that such false teachers were not yet in Rome. See, e. g., W. Sanday and A. C. Headlam, *A Critical and Exegetical Commentary on the Epistle to the Romans* (Edinburgh: T. & T. Clark, 5th edition, 1977) 429; also, more recently, Leon Morris, *The Epistle to the Romans* (Grand Rapids: Eerdmans, 1988) 539.

6. I Jn. 2:19 contains an important reminder that not everyone who appears to be part of the fellowship actually is. Our fellowship, as John makes clear in 1:1-4, is based on our common faith, and it is not impossible to have people in our midst who, while outwardly holding church membership, do not share our faith.

7. Some suggest that this was the reason why the Corinthians had failed to do anything about the incestuous man in their midst (I Cor. 5:1-8).

FOR THOUGHT AND DISCUSSION

I. Should the discipline of false teachers be a congregational or a brotherhood-wide matter? Explain your answer.

2. Provide some possible scenarios of "rejecting" a false teacher on both a personal and a congregational level. Be as specific as possible.

3. Why does Paul not discuss warning false teachers before rejecting them (Romans 16:17)? Is this inconsistent with his teachings elsewhere?

4. What suggestions can you add to the list of ways to reject false teaching without developing a "head-hunter" mentality?

5. Do you think that churches generally have been more ready to discipline in cases of moral failure or doctrinal error? Why?

"First, then, in order to be a good shepherd, the Elder must exercise the utmost care to prevent individual sheep from straying away from the flock; and when one, as it sometimes will, eludes all vigilance and strays away, he is to be prompt and energetic in going out to search for it and bring it back."

— J. W. McGarvey, *The Eldership*

WHAT ABOUT THE ELDERS?

During an interview with some elders and deacons of a church of almost two thousand members, I asked if the church practiced discipline. I was stunned by the reply from one of the elders: "We've never needed to." This comment told me a great deal, not only about the church he represented, but also about his concept of "eldering." It also highlights what I consider to be the number one problem concerning elders and the practice of discipline: most never even think of leading the church in discipline as being part of their role, and churches generally don't practice what they aren't *led* to practice.

Another serious problem with our thinking about elders which likewise hinders us from discipline is illustrated in the scenario of the Blank Street church (see Introduction: What's Wrong With This Picture?). You will notice that the disciplinary process at Blank Street, as is usually the case, was something which was initiated and carried out almost entirely by the elders, with prodding from the preacher. They decided that discipline must be done; they decided the criteria for who would be disciplined; they set the procedure to be followed; they made the contacts with the erring; they announced the outcome of the "restoration" efforts — and they received the blame for the confusion which resulted!

Unfortunately, both of the scenes described above have been repeated all too often. What's wrong with them? What *is* the responsibility of the elders in church discipline? And how can they function in ways that will make discipline more effective than it usually is?

Not Just the Elders

By now I hope that you've noticed that the texts which speak of discipline *always address the church as a whole* — not just the elders, or any other specific group within the congregation. No one is singled out in these texts as having the exclusive, or even primary, responsibility for church discipline.

Let's review a bit. When Jesus spoke of discipline in Matthew 18:15-17, he instructed his disciples generally, "If your brother sins, go and tell him his fault. . . ." *Every* disciple of Jesus bears the responsibility to care enough for the soul of an erring brother or sister to confront lovingly when sin is apparent. And if the erring person cannot be regained by private effort, gradually others are brought into the picture, until finally the entire church is informed and enlisted in the attempt to reclaim. And if such cannot be done, then it is the responsibility of everyone to "let him be to you as a Gentile and a tax collector." It is essential that everyone, as far as possible, be involved in the attempt to restore and, if necessary, in the ostracism which both protects the church from further harm and hopefully will yet turn the heart of the one disciplined.

Likewise, it is Paul's consistent practice to speak to the *entire church* about disciplinary matters — not just the elders or other leaders. As we learned from Galatians 6:1, "you who are spiritual" is not a distinct group within the Galatian churches, but the church as a whole, all of those who, unlike the sinning Christian, are "walking by the Spirit" rather than yielding to the flesh. Paul holds the entire Corinthian congregation accountable for the toleration of the incestuous man (I Cor. 5:1-8); in solemn assembly the church as a whole must "deliver him to Satan." And later, when he repents, all must forgive him, or else he may come to worse spiritual harm and the church suffer by being defrauded by Satan (II Cor. 2:5-11). In the same way, all of the Thessalonians are called upon to keep away from the disorderly and to warn them of the consequences of their misconduct (I Thess. 5:14, II Thess. 3:6-15). And the Roman church is exhorted as a body to watch out for and turn away from those whose teachings were in opposition to what they had already received (Rom. 16:17-18).

The only exceptions to speaking to the church as a whole are those letters which are addressed to Paul's associates, Titus and Timothy. In these cases, Paul naturally speaks to his apostolic representatives in the singular, but we should not conclude that there are individuals in the church today with the same authority to act single-handedly in an authoritarian manner. Timothy and Titus were appointed apostolic representatives. Likewise, that these letters were preserved by the churches with which Titus and Timothy labored, and that the church today still regards them as normative for the church as a whole, suggests that discipline is, even in these letters, the concern of the entire body and not just the leaders of it. The same principle holds true in I John 4:1ff, where John makes "testing the spirits" the obligation of the entire church. And when Jesus scolds the churches of Pergamum and Thyatira for their tolerance of false teachers and compromisers (Rev. 2:12-29), he speaks to the congregations as units (represented by their "angels"),[1] and adds the solemn warning: "He who has ears, let him hear what the Spirit says *to the churches.*"

Leadership in Discipline

But in spite of all of this, it would be a serious mistake to think that the elders of the church have no special role in administering discipline. Common sense would require that someone must take the lead in discipline, especially when formal actions (such as the withdrawal of fellowship or congregation-wide warnings against false teachers) become necessary. Some very delicate decisions must be made in such cases, and who would be better suited to make them than the church's shepherds, those charged with the responsibility to look after the spiritual welfare of the entire congregation? It is not wrong to look to the elders to provide such leadership; it *is* wrong to conclude that no action can be taken until it is taken by one or more of the elders. The texts discussed above, especially Matthew 18:15-17 and Galatians 6:1, indicate that *any* of us can (and *should*) begin the effort to restore whenever we become aware of the need for intervention. But once the process is begun and a wider circle of intervention is called for, we would hope that the elders would take the lead in trying to reclaim a lost sheep.

Although there are no Scriptures which make the elders *exclusively* responsible for discipline, there are Biblical indications that they have a special responsibility in this regard. It was to the elders/overseers of the Ephesian church that Paul said, "Take heed to yourselves and to all the flock, in which the Holy Spirit has made you overseers. . ." (Acts 20:28). It is the elders who are warned of the coming of wolves against whom the church must be protected, and they are told to "care for" (literally, "shepherd") the church of God. Likewise, Paul reminds Titus that he had left him in Crete to "appoint elders in every town" (Tit. 1:5). A few verses later one of the primary reasons for the need for such leaders is emphatically stated: "he must hold firm to the sure word as taught, so that he may be able to give instruction in sound doctrine and also to confute those who contradict it. For there are many insubordinate men, empty talkers and deceivers. . . they must be silenced. . ." (1:9-11). The Cretan elders were not appointed to function as a board of directors or decision-makers for the church. They were appointed to teach the faith and to protect the church from trouble-makers. Although Paul does not specifically mention the elders in giving his instructions about the divisive person (3:10-11), it follows logically from the context of the letter that the elders should take the lead in this. Otherwise, who would make the decision that someone had become so opinionated as to require correction in cases involving the entire congregation, if not those charged with the responsibilities of teaching and protecting the church? In the same way, Hebrews 13:17 teaches us to submit to our "leaders" (without specifying elders), "for they are keeping watch over your souls, as men who will have to give account." Anyone who has the primary responsibility for the care of souls must of necessity have primary responsibility for discipline.

It is sad that so few elders in today's church recognize their role as having anything to do with discipline. Unfortunately, we have ignored the plain words of Scripture and distorted the Biblical role of elders, so that men frequently assume these positions with no thought of leading the church in discipline, and congregations generally don't expect it of them. We are suffering in churches of Christ from a critical lack of genuine spiritual leadership, men who see themselves as shepherds entrusted with the responsibility of God's church, a responsibility for which they will have to answer before God's throne. We have traditionally shied away from the terms "pastor" and "shepherd" in referring to our elders, and the truth is that in most churches there isn't a great deal of pastoring or shepherding going on. This is having disastrous consequences for the church all across America. Numerous congregations are facing crises of spiritual weakness, false teaching, immorality, and disunity. And in most cases we don't have the spiritual leadership to cope with these problems. Our "boards" of elders are generally prepared to make decisions about budgets, buildings, and personnel, but are not at all prepared to protect the church from the ravages of sin. Elders need to spend more time studying Ezekiel's stinging indictment of the negligent shepherds of Israel, who did everything well except feed the sheep (Ezek. 34), and our Lord's words in John 10 concerning the hirelings who run when the wolf appears rather than standing firm to protect the flock from danger. Those who wear the title of "elders" must take seriously the task of feeding (teaching, encouraging) the church and protecting it from harm (including discipline, when necessary). God allows no one to assume that name without also expecting them to be shepherds.

This is not intended as a blanket indictment of elders, many of whom are doing their best to lead God's people as his word directs, but as a fervent plea for more elders to recognize their God-given role as shepherds. I stated in the Introduction that we are suffering from a serious lack of discipline in churches of Christ, and few would argue with this. *Nothing is likely to change until our elders begin to lead us in the right direction*!

What If There Are No Elders?

A question frequently asked is, "Can a church practice discipline if it has no elders?" Because we generally assume that discipline is solely an "elder function," we normally answer this question in the negative. As a result, churches without elders frequently languish under situations where discipline is badly needed. But I'm convinced that this is a false assumption. Since discipline is never specified to be an "elder function," but a *congregational* function and an *individual* function, it follows that a church — and even an individual — can practice discipline in the absence of elders. Actions such as going privately to a brother do not require anyone else's input or participation, and we can certainly take two or three others with us without elder involvement. It may be more difficult to "tell it to the church" and withdraw from someone without the leadership of elders, but even this can be done. One of the most effective instances of congregational discipline which I have ever personally witnessed was in a church of forty adult members with no elders, which effectively confronted, withdrew from, and restored an adulterous member. The decision was virtually unanimous among the members, and the congregation participated fully in both the decision and the action itself. We should not allow ourselves to think that the absence of elders excuses us from discipline.

A similar question involves situations in which there *are* elders, but they refuse to act even when circumstances clearly call for congregational discipline. It often happens that members of a congregation will be aware of·a situation requiring disciplinary action and will bring it to the attention of the elders, only to be ignored. What can an individual Christian do in such cases, without being insubordinate toward the elders or causing division within the congregation? Again, we should note the personal responsibility given to each of us by Jesus himself: "If your brother sins, go and tell him his fault. . . ." And Paul's words to the Galatian churches: ". . .you who are spiritual restore such a one. . . ." The collective responsibility of the church as a whole begins with the actions of concerned individuals. Such personal expressions of concern about our brother or sister's welfare ought to be going on all the time, with no thought to what others will or will not do. And even if the elders refuse to act in a given situation, that does not prevent the individual from personally withholding fellowship from a sinning member or false teacher.[2] Again, it is extremely important that, except in the extreme kinds of cases noted in the preceding chapters, we not short-circuit the process described in Matthew 18. We should go personally and privately to the sinning brother or sister and then take others with us. This will hopefully prevent us from acting hastily or unfairly and will help us know what we should do personally, regardless of whether the process goes any further.[3]

But we are not excused from trying to restore an erring brother or sister because others will not participate with us, any more than we would be excused from trying to lead others to Christ for the same reason. There are churches in which elders will not lead in evangelism, but that does not mean that there can be none. There are churches where the physical needs of the poor are ignored, but that does not excuse the individual Christian from doing what he/she can to minister to those needs (read Matt. 25!). We must individually accept our responsibility for the spiritual welfare of fellow-believers, regardless of what others do or don't do — even the elders. When this happens more and more in our churches, then perhaps we *will* begin to have more men emerge as elders who are willing to lead the church in discipline, because it is something in which they have been engaged already. Again, fellowship enters the picture: when our fellowship is genuine, discipline will naturally follow among *all* members. And such churches will produce godly leaders who know that one of their primary responsibilities is to enhance that fellowship and preserve the church's holiness through discipline.

Elders Are Not Exempt

Before we leave the subject of the elders' role in discipline, we should give some attention to a text which is generally overlooked, both in discussions of discipline and of elders. In I Timothy 5:19-21, Paul instructs Timothy,

> Pay no attention to an accusation against an elder, except "on the evidence of two or three witnesses." Rebuke those who are sinning in the presence of all, so that the rest will have fear. I charge you before God and Christ Jesus and the elect angels, to keep these (instructions) without bias, not playing any favorites.
>
> (Author's Translation)

This text is a much-needed reminder that the elders themselves are subject to the discipline of the church. They are not a hierarchy who dispense discipline to the rest, but shepherds of the flock who are likewise accountable to the "Chief Shepherd" (I Pet. 5:4) and to their brothers and sisters, and who experience the same weaknesses and temptations as all other Christians. Therefore they must be "shepherded," too, even to the point of discipline when necessary.

Paul's initial point in this context is that elders not be treated unfairly, since their role within the church places them in a vulnerable position as the objects of criticism and accusations. Following the Mosaic rule of "two or three witnesses" (Deut.

19:15), random accusations of wrong-doing are to be ignored. Unfair criticisms are inevitable, and if all of them were to be taken seriously, no one could function as an elder. But when two or three *do* confirm an accusation of wrong-doing, it's a different matter. When an elder *is* sinning,[4] his behavior ought not to be ignored, in spite of his position. *No role of leadership in the church can be construed as a license for sinful behavior.*[5]

Sinning elders, Paul says, are to be rebuked "in the presence of all." The question is, "all of whom?" There are two possibilities: "in the presence of the whole church,"[6] or "in the presence of all of the elders."[7] Likewise, does "the rest" who are to stand in fear as a result of this action mean "the rest of the church," or "the rest of the elders"? This is not an easy question, nor is it an unimportant one. On the basis of context, since Paul's immediate topic of discussion is elders, I prefer the latter interpretation, although the language could admittedly go either way. But remember that the main point is that there is to be no partiality; elders' sins are to be taken no more lightly nor seriously than those of other Christians. Assuming that the principles of Matthew 18:15-17 are to be followed in the case of elders, as of anyone else, then rebuking them in the presence of the whole church or in the presence of all the other elders should surely be preceded by attempts to restore them privately. I would be extremely hesitant to conclude that elders who sin, on the basis of two or three witnesses, should be brought before the church without first having been confronted privately.[8] If "in the presence of all" means before the entire congregation, then we should conclude that the principles of Matthew 18 are being assumed without being stated. In the case of elders, as of every other Christian, the goal is restoration and healing. Their special role as shepherds does not exempt them from such action, nor should the consideration due to any brother or sister be withheld in their case.

A Tribute to Elders

Shepherding the people of God in a local congregation can be an exhausting, time-consuming, frustrating, and thankless task. Of course, it has its share of rewards, but at best it is difficult business. I hope that what I've said in this chapter will be taken in the spirit in which it is intended: not as a criticism of elders, but as a prodding of our collective conscience to insist on the kind of spiritual leadership which the Scriptures say that we should have. *Elders are probably the single most decisive human factor in whether or not churches of Christ will ever repent of our indifference regarding discipline.*

As stated in the introduction, in writing this book I have a special concern for our godly elders who are charged above all others with the responsibility to shepherd the flock. Several years ago I presented some of this material to a class at one of our Christian university lectureships. It was attended mostly by elders. After the final session, several of them approached me and, with tears in their eyes, urged me to get this material in print. Their motive: "We know we need to lead the church in discipline, but we need help." I pray that they will find the help they need, whether in these pages or elsewhere. And I salute them for their shepherds' hearts.

1. A common interpretation of the "angels" of the seven churches is that they are the "pastors" of the individual churches (see, e. g., Ray Summers, *Worthy Is the Lamb* [Nashville: Broadman, 1951] 105, 109). But it seems more likely that the "angels" in some sense represent the churches themselves, since it is clear in each letter that Christ is addressing the church as a whole, not just an individual leader. "The Jews had long since become accustomed to the idea that each nation had its angelic representative in heaven, who presided over its fortunes and was held accountable for its misdeeds, and John is simply adapting this familiar notion to a new situation" (G. B. Caird, *A Commentary on the Revelation of St. John the Divine* [London: Adam & Charles Black, 1966] 24.

2. It should be noted that in Matt. 18:17 the phrase "to you" is singular. Some conclude that this means *only* an individual action of "letting him be to

you as a Gentile and tax collector." But this does not follow, since the problem has already been brought before the whole church. The singular "to you" merely emphasizes the responsibility of the individual believer — *all* individual believers.

3. Notice also that Paul's instructions to Timothy and Titus concerning discipline do not presume the participation of others. Hopefully the whole church would follow their lead, but they can and must act regardless of what others do or do not do.

4. The elder's "sinning" is expressed by a present active participle, denoting not something of which he was once guilty, but an on-going situation for which there has been no repentance. See NASB: "those who continue in sin"; RSV: "those who persist in sin." G. W. Knight III, however, thinks the participle signifies not persistent sin but present guilt, a distinction which in my opinion is difficult to sustain (*The Pastoral Epistles: A Commentary on the Greek Text* [Grand Rapids: Eerdmans, 1992] 236).

5. Although Paul doesn't specify it, the same could certainly be said of preachers, deacons, teachers, missionaries, and everyone else within the body.

6. Some translations bias our understanding of Paul's words by translating *enopion panton* ("in the presence of all") as "in public" (REB) or "publicly" (JB, NIV). Knight (236-37) and Donald Guthrie, *The Pastoral Epistles* (Grand Rapids: Eerdmans, 1957) 106, agree with this interpretation.

7. This is the interpretation favored by the majority of commentators, including Walter Lock, *A Critical and Exegetical Commentary on the Pastoral Epistles* (Edinburgh: T. & T. Clark, 1924) 63; J. W. Roberts, *Letters to Timothy* (Austin, TX: Sweet, 1964) 60; A. T. Hanson, *The Pastoral Epistles* (Grand Rapids: Eerdmans, 1982) 102-03; and William Hendriksen, *New Testament Commentary: Exposition of the Pastoral Epistles* (Grand Rapids: Baker, 1957) 183.

8. I cannot concur with the opinion of Hendriksen, who maintains that an elder's sin is to be "punished even more severely than that of others" (183). This seems to miss Paul's point that there should be no partiality.

FOR THOUGHT AND DISCUSSION

1. In what ways does the New Testament teach that discipline is the responsibility of all Christians, and not just of the elders?

2. Why and in what ways are elders in a position of special responsibility where discipline is concerned? Explain specifically what you think their responsibility is.

3. Discuss the subject of discipline with one or more elders in your congregation. How important is it in their thinking? What role does discipline play in their conception of what it means to be an elder?

4. Imagine that you are a member of a church with no elders, and you become aware of a serious situation requiring disciplinary action. No one else knows about it. How would you proceed?

5. Do you think that elders who continually sin should be (initially, at least) rebuked in the presence of the other elders, or in the presence of the whole church? Why? Have you ever seen an elder disciplined? How was it done, and what was the outcome?

"To abandon discipline because it has sometimes been ill-administered is as unwarranted as it would be to abandon worship on the ground that it has sometimes been ill-conducted. The relaxation of discipline has often more absurd results than ever attended its excess."

— Geddes MacGregor, *The Coming Reformation*

QUESTIONS, QUESTIONS

I have no delusions that what I have said so far will answer all of the questions which might be asked about this important subject. Situations requiring discipline can vary in many ways, and each case must be dealt with individually. There are many variables — and therefore, many questions.

Two works with which I am familiar deal at length with a variety of frequently-asked questions, and generally do so quite well, so I see no need to repeat their efforts. I am referring to the book by J. Carl Laney, *A Guide to Church Discipline* (Minneapolis: Bethany), 1985, and to the booklet by Flavil R. Yeakley, Jr., "Questions and Answers About Church Discipline," which is described on its cover as "Biblical and practical answers to the 25 questions most frequently asked concerning church discipline in general and specifically concerning the case of Guinn vs. the Collinsville Church of Christ." Both of these address a variety of questions in a sensitive and thought-provoking way, and although I do not always agree with their answers, I highly recommend them for your consideration.

Some of the questions discussed by Laney and Yeakley have

already been covered in previous chapters. What I want to do in this chapter is discuss a select few which I have not previously addressed, but which are of such practical importance that our study would be incomplete without dealing with them. Most of these will require a considerable amount of thought, prayer, and study to answer adequately. What I offer here is by no means infallible, but a mixture of applied Biblical principles, common sense, and opinion.

1. *Should people who have been "disfellowshipped" be allowed to attend worship services and partake of the Lord's Supper?*

The reality is that because worship services are something of a public event, it's difficult, if not impossible, to prohibit anyone from attending (except, perhaps, in a house church setting). And, as Laney points out, even if we wanted to prohibit a disciplined member from being present in the assembly, attempting to "evict" someone would likely produce nothing more than embarrassment and a media event. What is important is not whether the disciplined person attends, but what happens when he/she does so, and what associations other members have with him/her outside the assembly.

There are even some positive advantages to the person's attending. It may be that the process of self-examination at the Lord's Supper and hearing the word preached and taught will produce a willingness to repent. Also, the disciplined one's presence provides an opportunity for others to re-address the need for repentance, and if a disfellowshipped person is present, this certainly should happen. Most likely, if it does happen each time he/she attends, there either will be repentance, or attendance will cease

It is extremely important, however, that the church as a whole not act as if nothing is wrong and continue to socialize with one who has been disfellowshipped. To do so would render the church's action meaningless and encourage the offender to remain in sin. All contacts, whether at worship or otherwise, should be used as occasions to encourage repentance.

2. *Can the church withdraw fellowship from someone who is no longer attending worship?*

I have frequently heard the argument that, in such cases, a withdrawal would be meaningless, since the sinning Christian "has already withdrawn fellowship from the church," and "there is nothing left for the church to withdraw." This reasoning betrays an extremely inadequate understanding of "fellowship." It implies that fellowship only takes place in our assemblies. In some cases, this may be the reality of the situation, but usually it isn't. Many people who practice sin habitually and stop attending worship continue to associate with other Christians in business and social situations. To fail to go through with the withdrawal process when it is clearly called for, simply because someone has stopped attending worship, would be a serious failure to recognize the true nature of fellowship and the realities of sin.

Even in situations where the sinning Christian knows that disciplinary action is imminent and withdraws membership from the congregation first, there is a need for the church to follow through, so that members will know of the offender's relationship to the congregation and the reason for withdrawal of membership. Otherwise, the congregation may continue to associate freely with someone with whom they should not. In such cases, the announcement to the church would be somewhat different than in a situation involving a current member, but it should be done nonetheless. An additional reason for this would be to insure that the church does not appear to sanction the person's behavior in the eyes of the community by doing or saying nothing about sins committed by one who was a member there.

3. *What should Christians do when a family member has been withdrawn from?*

This is a very difficult area, and in the absence of more specific guidelines from Scripture, conscience and prayer must serve as our guide. In most cases, it would seem that family obligations should not be side-stepped in cases of withdrawal, particularly in situations involving a spouse. A husband or wife could continue normal family relations, it seems, while expressing disapproval of the other's behavior. This would not seem to be very different from living with a spouse who is not a Christian (I Cor. 7:12-13, I Pet. 3:1-6). In cases of more distant relationships, or where the offending family member is no longer a member of the household (as in the case of grown children), the same avoidance should probably be practiced as with any other erring Christian. There could be necessary exceptions to this, however, and we should be careful about passing judgment on people about how they handle it.

4. *Should other congregations be notified when someone has been withdrawn from?*

Again, this is very much a matter of judgment. As pointed out in our discussion of Matthew 18:15-17, discipline should be kept as private as possible. We should seriously consider, therefore, what purpose is to be served by informing other congregations of our disciplinary actions. If we are aware that a disciplined person has begun attending another congregation, then certainly that church should be made aware of the circumstances, so that they, too, can join in the efforts to restore, rather than unwittingly encouraging someone to continue in sin. This would seem to be a wiser course of action than sending out a general mailing to all area congregations.

5. *Is it really necessary for a public announcement of sin and/or withdrawal to be made?*

Because of the fear of lawsuits and other possible repercussions, we sometimes wonder if "telling it to the church" might not be accomplished in some other way than a public announcement. While in some extreme situations it might seem advisable to inform the church of someone's sin by means other than a public announcement (perhaps by mail), "telling it to the church" would seem to require doing so publicly. "Telling it to the church" is not merely a matter of giving out information; it is a communal occasion for mourning and for enlisting the aid of everyone in reclaiming a lost brother or sister. At least in the case of the incestuous man who was to be "delivered to Satan" (I Cor. 5:1-8), Paul specified that the action was to be carried out "when you are assembled together." There is something about the solemn assembly of the church for disciplinary purposes that cannot be matched in any other way. Again, we must not forget that discipline is an expression of fellowship.

On the other hand, "publicly" need not mean a meeting at which visitors and young children are present. There could be a special called meeting for this purpose. One way of doing it is to ask at the close of a service for visitors to leave and members to remain while a matter of great importance is discussed. Such a meeting would probably not be long, and visitors could be asked to wait in the foyer. Some object to this as insensitive to visitors, who are likely to take offense or be confused about what is taking place. My experience has been that this is *our* anxiety; visitors generally understand that not everything that takes place in a church family is their business. Often upon learning later what the meeting was about, they will express admiration for the seriousness with which sin is taken. I am sympathetic with the desire for our assemblies to be "visitor friendly," but this can be taken too far. The church does not assemble primarily for the benefit of visitors, but in order to do the will of God. Dealing adequately with sin in our midst must take precedence over impressing visitors.

6. *Must the specific sin be told to the congregation, or is it sufficient simply to say that someone has "sinned"?*

This is another sticky one. Some situations are so delicate and may involve hurting others to the extent that it might seem best not to specify what sin has been/is being committed. On the other hand, asking the church to withdraw its fellowship without knowing why can seem presumptuous and unfair. If the situation is already widely known, as in the case of the incestuous Corinthian, it would hardly be necessary to rehearse the details. But in many situations, if the attempt to restore has been handled as discreetly as it should have been, the congregation may be completely unaware of the circumstances. Generally, I would say that the sin should be named, at least in a generic way. For example, a sin could be labeled as "immorality" or "adultery" without naming the other party involved or any of the gory details. The purpose is not to satisfy the curiosity of the congregation but to deal realistically with sin. In extremely sensitive circumstances, however, it might seem appropriate for the elders to ask the church to trust their judgment in withdrawing fellowship from someone without knowing any specifics. But this would require a great deal of trust between the elders and the congregation.

7. *Doesn't withdrawing fellowship involve a kind of "judging" of others that is prohibited by Matthew 7:1: "Judge not, that you be not judged"?*

Jesus' teachings about not judging are some of the most misunderstood words in all the Bible. Verses 2-5 show that the concern is that we not be harsh and unloving in our judgments — that is, "judge not" equals "condemn not." Jesus is not teaching that we shouldn't be discerning about the rightness or wrongness of another's behavior. As a matter of fact, verse 6 admonishes us not to give dogs what is holy or cast our pearls before swine. This certainly implies that we must exercise some judgment as to who is a dog or a pig! Besides, other texts clearly teach us that we are not only allowed, but obligated, to make such judgments. After admonishing the Corinthians not to associate with sinning fellow-Christians, Paul writes, "For what have I to do with judging outsiders? *Is it not those inside the church whom you are to judge?"* (I Cor. 5:12). Likewise, I John 4:1ff instructs us not to believe every spirit (teaching) but to "test the spirits, to see if they are of God." We *must* be discerning about both the behavior and the teachings of others. Jesus' "judge not" certainly does not forbid the practice of discipline, nor does it excuse our failures to be as discerning as we ought to be.

8. *What about people who just stop attending? Should they be disfellowshiped?*

Again, opinions differ widely. What must be kept in mind is that failing to attend worship is a symptom of far deeper spiritual troubles. Something is clearly wrong with the discipleship of someone who never assembles with the church. Also, it should be the desire of every body of elders, and of the church as a whole, to keep track of *every member* and to be able to account for every one. Shepherding the flock would seem to require a knowledge of the whereabouts of the sheep, as well as some sense of their spiritual status.

It would seem, therefore, that in the case of people who cease to attend worship, some sort of disciplinary action is in order, if for no other reason than to keep the church informed. One of the important functions of discipline is what sociologists call "boundary maintenance" — determining who is "in" and who is "out." This does not necessarily mean judging who is saved and who isn't, but it means demarcating in some sense who is living up to community norms and who isn't. The Scriptures spell out clearly for us what the norms are, including attendance at worship. If someone consistently, over a long period of time and in spite of the efforts of others to teach them the importance of attending, simply refuses to come to church, something ought to be said to let this be known to the church as a whole. It need not be a "delivering to Satan, " but an informing of the congregation that this person is no longer attending and needs our prayers and admonitions to repent. The door would, of course, be left open to a return, but in the meantime the church realistically acknowledges that there is a problem. We should not be shy about stating openly that it is wrong to stop attending worship. To be silent on the matter while numerous members slip away could be construed as "silence giving consent."

In short, no one should ever exit our fellowship, for whatever reason, without some sort of statement to that effect. A church which never acknowledged members who moved away would be doing a poor job of keeping track of its membership. But, one which never acknowledges that some have *fallen* away is doing worse!

These and other possible questions highlight the truth that practicing discipline can be difficult. No one would deny that. It will require all of the wisdom, love, and sensitivity that we can muster to do it properly. But we should not allow such difficulties or unanswered questions to deter us from doing what is right. Surely the early congregations to whom the apostles wrote experienced many of the same questions and anxieties, and discipline was surely no less painful for them than for us.

But they were commanded to take a stand against sin and for their fellow-Christians, regardless of the difficulties involved. Only in this way can we hope to share God's holiness and enjoy his fellowship and that of our brothers and sisters for all eternity.

FOR THOUGHT AND DISCUSSION

1. What are the pros and cons of allowing a disfellowshiped person to attend worship?

2. In your opinion, can an individual Christian "withdraw fellowship from the church"? What should be the church's response when someone claims to have done this?

3. What suggestions can you offer concerning how a congregation can "tell it to the church" when a member requires congregational discipline?

4. Why is the practice of church discipline not a violation of Matthew 7:1? Why do you think this verse is so often raised in objection to discipline?

5. What does your congregation do in the case of members who stop attending? Is this a Biblical approach, based on what you have learned from this study? Why or why not? What do you think should be done?

"For the moment all discipline seems painful rather than pleasant; later it yields the peaceful fruit of righteousness to those who have been trained by it."

— Hebrews 12:11

WHERE DO WE GO FROM HERE?

As we come to a close, my prayer is that your heart has been moved to recognize the importance of discipline "that we may share his holiness." And not only to recognize it, but to be ready to do something about it, to put into practice the things taught so clearly in God's word.

But I realize that the practice of discipline has been so far removed from the thinking and experience of most of us that the thought of actually doing it seems overwhelming. Our minds are crowded with thoughts and fears of failure and dire consequences. What if we make a mistake? Will discipline really do any good? Won't people just be turned off from the gospel if we act so drastically in response to sin? What about lawsuits? Aren't we just going to get the church in trouble by practicing discipline? Can we really do this lovingly and effectively?

So where do we begin? How do we overcome the inertia which has been building among us for generations? Assuming that we are moved sufficiently by God's word, how do we get started? It won't be easy, but allow me to make a few suggestions.

1. *Begin with repentance.* If we are going to have God's blessings in carrying out the discipline which he requires, we must begin by repenting of our monumental failures in this

regard. Especially those who are church leaders — elders, preachers, and teachers — all who have a greater responsibility for the direction of God's people must acknowledge that our studied indifference to God's will is sin. We must confess that we've lost many more people to Satan than was necessary, that we've allowed our congregations to take sin less seriously than Scripture says that we should, that we've not sought the holiness without which no one will see the Lord, and that we've been content with a poor excuse for fellowship in many of our churches.

Part of our repentance must be the resolve to begin where we are and do better. Often when church leaders contemplate discipline, they are so overwhelmed by past failures that they become paralyzed, as if it were too late to do any good. How do we begin to discipline when we have failed to do so for so long? Where do we start? Start with the people under your care right now. You cannot correct the mistakes of the past or regain all of those once under your care. But you can resolve with God's help to do a better job with those you have now. If we recognize the mistakes of the past but are paralyzed from doing any better, our repentance is incomplete. And repentance must surely be the beginning point for all of us!

While such repentance needs to begin with our leaders, it isn't their sole responsibility. Individual Christians must develop the habit of watching out for one another's welfare and going to others when sin arises. In some cases, we may have to "lead our leaders" in the right direction. *All* of us must acknowledge our responsibility for discipline

2. *Trust God.* Many of our failures to discipline are traceable to one cause — fear. And the antidote to fear is *faith*. We must trust God that following his word *will* do good! And that no matter how frightening the prospects of taking sin seriously, God will be in control and will bless us. And that people will not be "turned off" by a church which takes its holiness seriously, but will be "turned on" by a church which does more than just *talk* about holiness. Let's face it. Our responses to God's will regarding discipline have betrayed a lack of faith. But if we will

"trust and obey," we will be amazed at how God will bless us.

Our often-expressed fear of lawsuits says more than we care to admit about our attitude toward obedience to God. Ever since the case of the Collinsville, Oklahoma church, the vast majority of our discussions of discipline have dealt with the legal aspects — mostly about how to avoid lawsuits. While this is a legitimate concern, it should hardly be the church's *first* concern. Our first concern should be obedience to God. We may, in fact, suffer financially (or in other ways), but since when does that justify failure to obey? Are we, as John White and Ken Blue suggest, more concerned about what is expedient than about what is right?[1] It is ironic that we have become so panicked over the legal question. Few among us are practicing enough congregational discipline to be in any danger!

J. Carl Laney tells a story about a little boy whose toy boat was blown far out of his reach into the pond where he was sailing it. Seeing his desperate attempts to retrieve it, an elderly gentleman came to help. Much to the little boy's horror, the old man began throwing rocks in the direction of the boat. But the boy soon saw the strategy. His friend threw the rocks beyond the boat, so that the ripples would drive it back to shore. What had appeared to him to be a destructive action was actually just what was needed to accomplish his objective. Likewise, discipline may appear destructive and counter-productive to us, but our Father knows what he's doing — and what we need to do. Trust him.

3. *Recognize the positive power of discipline.* God would not teach us to do something that is useless or destructive for the church. But our fears cause us to respond as if discipline were both useless and destructive. Much of our reasoning in this regard is simply false.

Take, for example, the often-heard complaint that practicing discipline will drive people away from the church. Nothing could be further from the truth! John White and Ken Blue rightly argue that people go away from the church, not because of the practice of discipline, but due to the *lack* of it. "Churches have become hospitals where sin-sick souls are given aspirin and entertainment to distract them from the diseases of their souls. God forgive us, we are more concerned with numbers than with holiness."[2] Joan Burge cites the example of St. Matthew Lutheran Church in Holt, Michigan, which practices discipline consistently. Members who stop attending and refuse counseling and restoration are declared to be "self-excommunicated." And the congregation has grown from 100 to 1600 members in a span of only ten years![3] Why is it that in many instances our religious neighbors are more readily grasping the positive benefits of church discipline than we are? While we are still largely ignoring the subject, many of them are advocating and practicing it, and reaping the benefits.

Francis Schaeffer observes that the lack of discipline has caused the church to lose power, purity, purpose, and integrity. He particularly enlarges on the last point: our witness to a skeptical world is severely damaged when all we do about sin is *talk*, while we tolerate its presence among us.[4] But if we show the world that we take both holiness and sin seriously, we will regain the integrity which we have lost, and our efforts at evangelism will bear more fruit than we have dared imagine.

4. *Develop a genuine sense of fellowship and pastoral care.* Because discipline is an expression of fellowship and is the responsibility of all Christians, these two items go hand-in-hand. We need a closer fellowship in which all members take responsibility to watch out for one another, where we "go to one another" about sin readily and as a natural expression of our love and concern. As mentioned earlier, until there is genuine fellowship, there can be no effective church discipline. Discipline outside the context of fellowship is what has produced some of the disasters of the past and why the whole subject of discipline has left a bad taste in the mouths of many who have witnessed its abuse. We must work hard at creating a climate of love, trust, and interaction among our members. Discipline will then flow naturally.

In order for this to happen, though, we need to restore genuine *pastoral leadership* in our congregations. Churches need to insist that elders truly shepherd the flock, not just "make decisions." We need to appoint men less for their business expertise and more for their shepherds' hearts. Such men will lead the way and set the example of genuine concern, and in turn they will be able to lead the church in corporate disciplinary action when necessary. As I hope you can see by now, restoring the practice of church discipline means restoring not just one ancient Christian practice, but some fundamental characteristics of the church which we have been lacking.

5. *Teach the church.* Many are so devoid of understanding what Scripture teaches about discipline that it would be disastrous to try to begin practicing it. There is a serious need for teaching about all aspects of discipline, beginning with the fundamental issues of sin, holiness, and fellowship, and proceeding to more specific concerns, such as how to confront lovingly about sin and what Scripture says about withdrawing fellowship.

Mark Littleton identifies five problems which make the practice of church discipline difficult:

1. People wonder whether it will do any good.
2. No one is clear about what sins we are to discipline.
3. People fear the outcome.
4. People associate discipline with excommunication and intolerance.
5. People have few models of positive discipline to reflect on.

In response, he suggests five practices that create a healthy disciplinary environment:

1. A clear understanding of sin and a desire for holiness.
2. Regarding church membership as a responsibility to love, admonish, encourage, and build one another up.
3. Practicing confession of sin on a personal level.
4. Teaching people how to admonish one another in love.
5. Follow-up and support for those who have sinned.[5]

As you can see, most of this reflects a need for teaching — not just about discipline *per se*, but about what it means to be the church. Our lack of discipline betrays a serious lack of understanding of who we are and what we are supposed to be about.

6. *Make holiness a priority.* The bottom line of discipline is whether we are serious about pleasing God and about reflecting the holiness which is inherent in his nature. We must wake up from our entertainment mentality and get back to talking about being God's holy people, with all that holiness entails. But we must do more than just talk. We must teach holiness, practice holiness, and discipline those who refuse to be holy. Going back to our original thesis, based on Hebrews 12:5-11, "God disciplines us for our good, that we may share his holiness." Partaking in the holiness of God ought to be the goal of every one of us, and we must recognize the essential role of discipline in that sanctification process. God disciplines us. We must discipline ourselves. And we must discipline each other.

May God bless us as we strive to share his holiness!

1. *Healing the Wounded: The Costly Love of Church Discipline* (Downers Grove, Illinois: InterVarsity Press, 1985) 30.

2. White and Blue, *Healing the Wounded*, 34.

3. Joan Burge, "The Church That Dares to Discipline," *Christian Life* August, 1980, Vol. 42 (No. 4) 26-27, 45-57.

4. Francis A. Schaeffer, *The Church Before the Watching World* (Downers Grove, Illinois: InterVarsity Press, 1971) 62ff.

5. Mark R. Littleton, "Church Discipline: A Remedy for What Ails the Body," *Christianity Today* May 8, 1981, 30-33.

FOR THOUGHT AND DISCUSSION

I. Which of the suggestions discussed in this lesson is a strong-point of your congregation? In which are you most lacking?

2. Can you think of some Bible examples of people who were called upon to do what seemed unreasonable and potentially destructive, yet were blessed by God for going ahead in faith?

3. How would your congregation be different if discipline were practiced consistently? Do you think you would find it a more attractive and helpful place spiritually, or less so?

4. Read Acts 5:1-14. What effect did God's discipline of Ananias and Sapphira have on the rest of the Jerusalem church? On those outside the church? What bearing, if any, does this have on the need for congregational discipline today?

5. What can you personally do to make holiness more of a priority in your own life? In the congregation where you worship?